JOHNNY APPLESEED
God's Faithful Planter—John Chapman
by David R. Collins

Young John was restless. It was hard to keep his mind on schooling and the farm chores. By 1792, when he turned eighteen, his feet were itching for travel. His father handed him a parting gift and said, "As long as you carry God's Word, your path will be straight." To Johnny, the Bible was a fitting treasure.

Although Johnny headed west, the roads he took weren't always straight. Leaving Massachusetts behind, he climbed mountains, followed dusty trails, floated down singing waterways, and wandered all over the newly settled wilderness.

In his knapsack he carried his Bible and as many apple seeds as he could stuff in. The only roots he knew were those he planted for others, the rich growing roots of seedling apple trees. He needed always to move, to cover ground, but he left behind a trail of apple trees for those who would later follow that same way.

People grew used to the sight of the thin barefooted man with his knapsack on his back and wearing his cooking pot for a hat. Johnny knew pioneer settlers, townfolk, Indians, and the wild critters of the outdoors. In time, everyone thought of him as Johnny Appleseed.

ABOUT THE AUTHOR

David Collins—teacher, author, speaker, a man of many talents—lives in Moline, Illinois. He has written at least twenty-five books and is still going strong. Other Sower Series books from his typewriter are *Abraham Lincoln, George Washington Carver, Francis Scott Key,* and *Florence Nightingale.*

Mr. Collins has been honored by many organizations, including the Junior Literary Guild, the National Book Council, and the Illinois Council of Parents and Teachers.

"When I write for young readers," says Mr. Collins, "I attempt to apply a 'double E' standard to my work. I hope to entertain and educate. I want my young readers to enjoy the experience of reading and take something away from it too, even if it's just one new word or one different idea."

ABOUT THE ARTIST

Joe Van Severen—who lives in West Chicago, Illinois—illustrated Sower Series books *George Washington Carver* and *Francis Scott Key.*

Mr. Van Severen says that Johnny Appleseed has always been a favorite of his. Of the pictures for this book, he says, "I had fun doing them."

Johnny Appleseed

God's Faithful Planter
John Chapman

by

David R. Collins

Illustrated by **Joe Van Severen**

MOTT MEDIA

Milford, Michigan 48042

All Scriptures are from the King James Version of the Bible.

Louise H. Rock, Editor
A. G. Smith, Cover Artist

LIBRARY OF CONGRESS CATALOGING IN PUBLICATION DATA

Collins, David R.
　　Johnny Appleseed: God's Faithful Planter, John Chapman.

　　(The Sowers)
　　Bibliography: p. 145
　　Includes index.

　　SUMMARY: A first-person narrative of the life of the legendary figure who traveled across the American frontier planting apple trees and carrying the Christian faith to pioneer families.
　　1. Appleseed, Johnny, 1774-1845—Juvenile literature. 2. Apple growers—United States—Biography—Juvenile literature. 3. Missionaries—United States—Biography—Juvenile literature. 4. Frontier and pioneer life—Middle West—Juvenile literature. [1. Appleseed, Johnny, 1774-1845. 2. Apple growers. 3. Missionaries. 4. Frontier and pioneer life. 5. Christian biography] I. Van Severen, Joe, ill. II. Title.

SB63.C46C65 1985　　　　634'.11'0924 [B] [92]　　　　84-60315
ISBN 0-88062-135-4 Hardbound
ISBN 0-88062-134-6 Paperbound

PREFACE

Did you happen to notice the imprint on the front of this book? It's on the left-hand corner of the cover. It is the figure of a planter sowing seeds as he walks.

This book is a part of the Sowers Series. The people in the Sowers Series accepted Jesus, God's Son, as Savior, and sowed seeds of faith and love to others. Wonderful people like Abraham Lincoln, Abigail Adams, George Washington Carver, Christopher Columbus, and others are included in the Sower Series.

Johnny Apleseed, whose real name was John Chapman, could easily have posed for the imprint on the cover of this book. Into the soil he sowed tiny appleseeds. With his loving care and God's help, the seeds soon became saplings, then sturdy trees with beautiful blossoms, and finally bountiful orchards.

And as he planted tiny seeds into the soil across an ever-growing America, Johnny Appleseed carried the Christian message to everyone he met. Some historians credit him with starting the first "Circulating library" because of the way he took his Bible from one homestead to another. He was truly a messenger of God, sharing the Lord's Word to all who would listen.

This story of Johnny Appleseed is written as he might have told it. Every effort has been made to separate facts and truth from the legends and myths which surround this American hero. You may travel with this man as he faces attacks by Indians and rattlesnakes, as he fights the rapids of a raging river, and as he encounters the ugliness of pride and hate.

And perhaps, just perhaps, you too may become a greater sower of Christian love and faith. Indeed, the world has room for many more.

David R. Collins
Moline, Illinois

CONTENTS

INTRODUCTION

Have you ever heard of John Chapman?

Probably not.

Have you ever heard of Johnny Appleseed?

Yes, that name is surely more familiar to you. Johnny Appleseed has long enjoyed a favorite place among the heroes of our land. Every child learns exciting tales of that legendary man who enriched frontier soil by sowing appleseeds long ago.

But Johnny Appleseed, or John Chapman, which was his Christian name, planted much more than seeds into soil. He carried the Word of God and the Christian faith to many pioneer families. Johnny planted apples because he saw them as "God's finest fruit." He shared God's Word because Johnny felt it was the best way of serving God on earth.

The life of Johnny Appleseed is a confusing mixture of fact and myth. Sifting through the imaginative tales created by story-tellers and the careful research of historians is no easy task. But what emerges is a life dedicated to faith and a burning desire to help others. This book traces that life, with every effort to be historically accurate.

To add a more personal dimension to the life of Johnny Appleseed, his story is told as a first person narrative. I hope this means of presentation will allow the reader to become part of the events as they occur.

David R. Collins
Moline, Illinois

Mystery Lady

"Johnny! My little Johnny boy."

I sat up straight in bed, gripping the heavy quilt around my neck. My heart thumped wildly. It was that dream again.

"Bess?" I whispered. "Are you awake?"

Across the room I heard my ten-year-old sister stir in her sleep. A tired voice mumbled, "What is it, Johnny?"

"Bess, I had that dream again. The mystery lady was here. Do you ever dream about her? I wonder—"

Suddenly the light of a candle appeared in the doorway. The flame flickered, casting dancing shadows around the room. I rubbed my eyes. When I put my hands down, I saw my father standing beside my bed. He put the candleholder on a nearby table and sat down.

"Now, Master John Chapman, what is it that keeps a six-year-old lad's tongue wagging at this hour of the night?"

My father's hand felt welcome to my cheek. I was

glad he was home. No longer did we have to fear the British guns and soldiers. They had left our Massachusetts colony and we were safe. Our country was free. All in all, 1780 was a good time to be alive.

Except for the dream.

Again and again the dream came to me. A woman stood on a hillside, surrounded by mist and clouds. She held an arm out to me, beckoning me to come to her. "Johnny," she called, "my little Johnny boy."

I told my pa about the dream. He pushed my hair off my forehead. His palm was rough. It was not easy being the best farmer in Longmeadow village, probably in all of Massachusetts. Every harvest time, Pa had the biggest and finest vegetables. He was a good carpenter, too. People came from miles away to buy his strong wheels, chairs, and tables. Yes, his hands were rough, but they felt warm and firm against my back and shoulders.

"Perhaps it is Lucy you see in your dream, boy."

I shook my head. No, I knew it was not Miss Lucy, Pa's new bride. She was young, only eighteen, and her red curls danced when she ran. The lady in the dream was older, with pale skin and dark hair.

"No, I don't think it is Lucy," I said.

Pa was silent for several moments. Then he spoke, almost in a whisper.

"You were just a small mite when your dear ma died, Johnny, only about three years upon this earth as I recall. But the lady in your dream just might be your mother, Johnny. She loved you and Bess more than anything."

Pa's voice sounded so far away.

"Was she pretty?"

"Oh, yes, boy. I can still see her, sitting beside the hearth, stitching and darning. The loveliest blue eyes and black hair."

"Pa, I *do* think it's Ma in my dreams. But where is she? Why did she have to die?"

"It was the Lord's wish, Johnny. Ma took sick right after having your wee brother Nathaniel. We lost the both of them." Pa stopped, gazing over at the flickering candle. "Now they're both with the Lord, in his world of glory."

I slipped deeper into my bed.

"But why does she come to me in my dreams?" I asked. "What does she want?"

Pa smiled. "It's a sign, lad. It's a sign from the good Lord that he wants you to be with Him, too." Pa hoisted the quilt around my neck. "Not for a time, though, I'm thinking. But someday, you'll be joining your good ma once again. I'm goin' to be there, too, Johnny, my lad."

My eyes suddenly felt heavy. Pa's voice sounded so far away. "Yes, Pa. All of us together—"

Pa was not the only one who spoke of the Lord's wishes. Each Sabbath morning, Pa, Mama Lucy, Lucy's ma whom we respectfully called Grandma Cooley, Bess, and I made our way to the meeting house. There we listened to Reverend Williams tell us the word of God and the story of our Lord. More wrinkles lined the good Reverend's face than barklines around the old oak near the schoolhouse. Sometimes when the Reverend spoke about the Lord, I wondered if the two of them had grown up together. The thought made me smile.

"Is Reverend Williams as old as the Lord?" I asked Pa one day as we returned from service.

"You'll not be poking fun at your elders," Pa answered sternly. "Age brings wisdom. Reverend Stephen Williams is one of the finest preachers in the entire Massachusetts colony. You'll gain no blessings with such foolishness. And you may find there's more than kindling fire that can be made from a cedar switch. A cedar switch can bring a strong sting to a small boy's backside.''

I knew well the tone of Pa's voice. In truth, I felt that strong sting more than once. It wasn't that I meant to anger Pa. But sometimes my words tumbled out before I knew they were gone. Other times I was late getting my chores done after school.

"Did you stop by the river this afternoon, boy?" Pa would ask.

"Yes, Pa. There was a flatboat passing along. I trailed it for an hour. Looked like a heavy load of fish and fur."

Miss Lucy shook her head. "Schoolmaster Doobs says you might be tending to your Dilworth Speller and your New England Primer a bit more," she offered. "All you boys are so taken by that river."

Yes, "taken" we all were. During the winter, we skated on the ice. In the spring, there was shad fishing. Nets were brought to the village common for mending. Once the catches were brought in, the fish were salted and given out to everyone for winter eating.

Not that school was all that bad. There was a special joy to working with figures and sums. Reading, too, brought me pleasure.

"The key to happiness in life is through reading," said Schoolmaster Doobs. "Once you can read by yourself, you can read the Holy Scriptures. They will carry you along the road to the world of glory in heaven."

And then there was the day the schoolmaster brought the apple.

We had been reading about the earth and the sun. But it was clear that not everyone in the schoolhouse understood how the two big worlds related to each other. We watched closely while Master Doobs left

the classroom. When he returned later, he carried a lighted candle.

"Imagine this candle is the sun," the schoolmaster said, setting the candleholder on his desk at the front of the room. He took a giant apple and held it high. "Now imagine this apple to be the earth."

There were a few light murmurs in the room, but no one laughed. It was clear that Schoolmaster Doobs wished complete silence and attention. He turned the apple in his hand.

"Just as I turn this apple in space, so too turns the earth. It shares the sun's warmth and light."

How clear it all became! Yet who controlled all this? How could these giant bodies move?

The schoolmaster had the answer. "And it is all done through the power of God," he explained. "Whatever we do, wherever we go, we are in His hands."

I watched as Schoolmaster Doobs blew out the candle's flame and set the apple back upon his desk. There was such a wonder to this world!

How eager I was to know more.

A Travelin' Song

As the years rolled along, the dream of the "mystery lady" came less often. Perhaps it was because there was so much happening in my life that other dreams took its place.

When I was thirteen in 1787, the leaders of our new country signed an official Constitution, and two years later it became law. General George Washington was elected the first President, an event that thrilled my father.

"There was no other choice," Pa declared. "Any of us who served with him in the Revolution know that. He'll pull the country together, just like he helped win us our freedom from England."

But there was still another reason the "mystery lady" may have disappeared. No one with an ounce of sense would have wanted to stay for an extra minute in our little house at Longmeadow. Pa and Lucy took to having babies, and the noise of crying infants and hollerin' young ones traveled for miles. Lucy called each new babe another "blessing from God," but I

confess I wished the Almighty might send His blessings with a bit less voice. Grandma Cooley spoke her
piece about the matter loud and clear.

"I'm a-gettin' out of this house," she declared one
night at the supper table, "while I've still a bit of my
hearin' left. I'll come back whenever you need me,
Nat and Lucy, but I jest can't listen to all this com-
motion every hour of the night and day. I believe I
would give away everything I own to enjoy one full
day and night without havin' to answer a baby's cry
or feed a squallin' mouth. I'm jest too old for such
things."

Grandma Cooley's words rang with truth, and I
was tempted to go with her if she'd have let me. But
it did not seem quite the decent thing to do, for both
of us to run away when there was so much work. But
I confess, my own long legs were gettin' eager to head
west. Every time I visited the river and watched those
flatboats carrying their loads, the urge grew stronger.

To help feed and clothe the new Chapman arrivals,
Pa turned out more and more wooden bowls, pails,
and spoons. I fixed up an old cart and rolled it along
dusty roads, selling Pa's woodenwares everywhere I
found an interested face. Pa and Lucy were grateful
for the extra coins I brought in. I enjoyed the traveling and wished more and more that I could feel free
and independent enough to head out for good.

But by 1792, when I turned eighteen, my feet got
to itching for travel so much I knew I had to get away.
The west was calling to me. My younger half brother
Nathaniel suffered from the same ailment.

"I don't care where you're headed," Nat told me.
"I am goin' with you. Pa will be grateful for two less
mouths to feed."

"That much is certain," I answered. "But you are
only eleven."

"I won't be a burden to you, Johnny." Nat puffed out his chest like a stuffed turkey, and he balanced tall on his feet. "I'm big for my age anyway."

I could not control my laughter. "Big you are, but not nearly as big as you'd have me think. Now get down off your toes before you fall, and let out your wind before you burst. If Pa gives permission, I'll take you along."

Nat was right. Much as Pa loved us both, and we loved Pa, Lucy, and the rest, two less mouths was a welcome fact in our home. Nat and I began packing a few bits of clothes and food.

We set out early one morning, our adventuresome spirits high.

As a parting gift Pa handed me a small Bible. A more fitting treasure I could not have asked for.

"As long as you carry God's Word, your path will be a straight one," Pa noted. "You and young Nathaniel share this Book often."

Pa could not have been more of a prophet. Nat and I headed west to my uncle's home in New York State. We found Uncle John's cabin, but my father's brother was nowhere in sight.

"I believe he headed across the Catskills," a neighbor told us, pointing to the mountaintops in the distance. "Seems everybody has the traveling urge."

Yes, traveling seemed to be in everyone's blood. Back at Longmeadow, the inns were always full of folks going to New York City or Boston. Talk of free open land drew others farther west, even past the towering Allegheny Mountains.

But as for Nat and me, we were content just to settle into Uncle John's cabin for the winter months. I would not have minded covering a few more miles, but Nat was only eleven. The Lord directed us older folks to look out for the younger ones. I did not want to pull Nat through any snowdrifts or ice storms.

"Don't you be babying me," Nat scolded. "I can do everything you can do."

I smiled. "That may be true enough, my friend. But if we were to hit a five-foot snow covering, I'd still be lookin' out over it. You'd be buried inside where not a soul could see the top of your head."

Uncle John's cabin proved a welcome hideaway from the wind and cold. He had left a hearty supply of vittles in the house, and Nat and I vowed to replenish what we ate before we bid leave in the spring.

There is nothing quite like a blazing hot fire in the wintertime. Often Nat and I cooked a mighty meal of biscuits and stew, then found cozy seats on the hearth. The Bible Pa sent along with me captured many an evening.

"Tell the story about how so many people were fed from just a few fishes and a few loaves of bread," Nat would beg.

The story of how Jesus made the blind man see was a special favorite as was the story of the proud man and the humble man who went to the temple to pray.

"We're likely to come out of this cabin as preachers in the spring," I teased Nat. "We'll know that Bible better than old Reverend Williams himself."

Nat shook his head. "No one knows the Bible as well as he does," the boy declared.

I knew Nat was right. But preachers or not, I knew the knowledge we were learning of the Holy Word would be a strength to us in the future.

By the time the spring thaws arrived, Nat was eager to return home. I took him back to our family pocket of safety in Longmeadow, but I did not stay long. There was more than a traveling urge in me. It was a fever, a burning desire to move further into this country and explore.

I was not alone in my desire to travel. Many families in the Connecticut Valley were packing up and heading west. When word arrived that the Holland Land Company was offering cheap land in Pennsylvania's Allegheny northwest, I bid my family farewell and again headed west.

There was no way of knowing what the winter of 1797 would bring in weather. As I trudged across the rich New England soil from New York into Pennsylvania, I found myself caught up in new ideas and new tasks to perform.

A new awareness of God came into my life. I sensed a greater purpose, as well. I remembered Psalm 126:6 which stated, "He that goeth forth and weepeth, bearing precious seed, shall doubtless come again with rejoicing, bringing his sheaves with him." Now and then on my travels, I had helped farmers plant their orchards. My heart felt lifted, knowing that the work I was doing added beauty and value to the earth God had created. There was joy in hard work, honesty in sweat and labor.

But still another urge seemed to plant its own seed within me. How exciting it would be to venture into the wilderness before the pioneers came ready to build a future. Would it not be a warm welcome to reach a land bursting with the richness of God's blessings and find fruit to fill empty stomachs and to strengthen weary bodies? Yes, I thought, yes. Surely there was a place for such a man accepting such a task.

It was just such a notion that led me to the Susquehanna region of Pennsylvania. I confess I was not always met with a cheerful welcome and "Good day, stranger." In truth, many an eye looked me over with suspicion. Not without some reason, I suspect. I never did hanker for shoes and boots. I like the good fresh air to reach my feet. Whether the ground be cold or

hot, the step is a mite quicker when the feet are bare.

Some folks probably thought my hat a bit peculiar as well. But a traveler needs to carry a good pewter pot for heating up vittles. Now and then I came to using the pot for a hat. And when my Bible grew a bit troublesome being carried in my pocket, I stuck it inside the pewter pot. Yes, Johnny Chapman coming to town probably was a sight to see. It did not make me change my ways though. I never did hold much to those who measured a man's worth by his appearance. I enjoyed the words of Isaiah 52:7: "How beautiful upon the mountains are the feet of him that bringeth good tidings." As I traveled, I carried the words of God in the Bible. What better tidings could one man show another?

I found no joy in being inside. I enjoyed working in the orchards, harvesting the treasures of God's making from sturdy branches. No sooner would I settle in a place than my feet would start itching to travel new roads. There was something about the rivers, too. Their waters seem to share a melody—a song urging me west. "You, Johnny Chapman, follow us. Let us take you to new lands," those waters seem to sing.

And I listened.

The melody grew louder.

I knew I had to answer it.

So I packed my buckskins, a blanket, and a tomahawk. In a knapsack I stuffed my Bible. I traded my wages from working in the orchards for a rifle, for it was said there were still angry Indians in the west. Pa's fighting friend from the Revolutionary War days, General Anthony Wayne, had driven most of them away, but bands of them still roamed freely. I had no desire to use a rifle, but folks told me a man without a gun was easy prey for the redskins.

Finally, I stuffed all the appleseeds I could into my knapsack. They protected the Good Book well and I could not help but think that no better nourishment for mind and body existed than what I carried in my knapsack. I recalled Schoolmaster Doobs spinning an apple around the lighted candle. How bright that apple was, just as God made the earth to be. What better calling for a man like myself than to venture into the wilderness and share the fruits of God's blessings?

So I trudged off, following the singing waterways, across the Pennsylvania soil. At times I camped along the shores of the Allegheny River, whispered to sleep by the soft waves against the banks. Emigrants sometimes welcomed me in for the night, eager to share food and conversation with a new face.

"Where are you bound for?" my hosts would ask.

"Nowhere special," I would answer.

I would look into startled and confused eyes.

"But what do you plan to do?" would be the next queston.

"Carry the Word of the Lord and the seeds of His goodness to new lands." Eagerly I reached for my knapsack. "I'll be happy to share a bit of both with you if you'd allow me."

Nods of agreement followed. Traveling preachers were scarce to the Pennsylvania wilderness, and apple-seeds were just as welcome. By many a hearth I shared the glorious tales of the Lord to willing listeners.

And of all the listeners, the most eager were the children. Their eyes widened as big as Pa's wooden bowls. They soaked in every word I spoke and asked questions when I'd finished. There was trust in their faces—honest, loving trust. It was a joy to share with them. In the morning I would pack up and be gone. No matter how kindly I was treated, the melody of the river and the woods sang too sweetly.

And though I saw the joy of family, and the beauty of children that grew from the joy, my heart told me that such a life was not mine. The only roots I would know were those I would plant for others, the rich growing roots of seedling apple trees. I needed always to move, to cover ground.

Cover ground I did, stopping only to look for a spot to sow my first seeds. I found such a spot on Big Brokenshaw Creek in the county of Warren. A century was coming to an end, and it lifted my spirits to know that the 1800's would be welcomed by fresh sprouts of green here in the Pennsylvania wilderness. Pioneers spilling out of the east would be greeted by full fruits of God's blessings.

I stayed in the territory for a while, carefully tilling the soil and tending the seeds and early arrival of my plants. Though I was willing to share my efforts with those unable to buy, I hoped that I might sell a few to those who could afford them. I had no wish to be a beggar and live off others. But there were few settlers in Warren County. It belonged to the elk, the buffalo, and the timber wolf. So I traveled down the Allegheny once more.

It was while I was scouting around the Erie region that I found greater fear than I had ever known. Dawn had broken early one morning. Having doused the campfire and gathered up my things, I suddenly became aware of noises a short distance away. My campsite was in a clearing and I shielded my eyes with my hand and gazed to the north. Scrambling down a hillside were eight Indians, their voices raised in wild yelps and loud cries.

Quickly I turned around. Surely there was something or someone near me who was the target of their attention. No, there was nothing. I gripped my rifle. What good was such a weapon against a pack of eight attacking redskins?

"Lord, I need your help." I mumbled as I turned
to flee. "Help me in this time of need!"

3

Beware of Indians

Quickly I scampered along the lowslung hillsides,
barely allowing my feet to touch the ground. Behind
me the air was filled with war shrieks and howling.

A stranger to the region, I had little notion where
my desperate flight was taking me. But looking ahead
I could see nothing except a giant lake. My escape
was cut off!

Glancing back and pausing to catch my breath, I
could see the Indians approaching. Like attacking red
ants they came, eager to devour a tasty meal. I
shivered, realizing *I* was the goal of their hunt.

Ahead of me the land rose slightly near the shore.
I speeded my steps. Along the shore I slipped off my
knapsack and shoved it into a hole. A nearby rock
provided a perfect covering for my buried treasure.

Not wasting a minute, I went leaping into the water
like a frantic frog.

Although I was a fair swimmer and a better
oarsman, I knew I could never get across the lake.
Also, there was no sign of a canoe or any other vessel.

But the shallows of the lake did offer a thick growth of cattails and reeds. Past experiences with rivers, lakes, and creeks made me aware of a possible solution to my troubles. Another glance at the Indian pack racing toward the shore told me I had few choices. Sinking to my knees, I reached out for a reed with an airpipe stem. How grateful I was for the forest of waterplants that hid me from sight. For the first time, I realized how cold the water was. But it mattered little. My pounding heart seemed to warm my entire body.

With a mighty intake of air, I submerged beneath the water level. I lay flat on my back on the floor of the shallows, breathing through the reed, whose tip rose into open air.

I waited. Waited and prayed.

"Lord, spare me from this fearful trouble. Allow me to serve Thee with the life You have given me. I shall be a servant of Your will."

Suddenly my thoughts stopped. Opening my eyes but a slit, for the water was dirty, I turned my head from side to side. I could see nothing.

But I could feel movement. Yes, the Indians were moving around nearby. I held the reed perfectly straight. My heart was thumping so loud I was sure it could be heard for miles. Seconds slipped into minutes.

And then the movement stopped.

Still I waited. My body grew stiff and numb with cold. My fingers and toes felt like icicles. "Go away!" my heart shouted to the savages. "Go away and leave me alone!"

I waited as long as I could. Then, when my head seemed as if it would explode, I slowly pulled myself to the surface of the water. If the Indians were still there, I was a goner. But I refused to be frozen alive underwater.

The shore of the lake was deserted. I rubbed my eyes, looking closely for any sign of movement. There was none. Pulling myself to a kneeling position, I again surveyed the banks of the river. Empty. The Indians must have tired of the hunt. Perhaps the water's cold had discouraged them. Whatever it was, I was grateful. As I made my way to shore, I gazed upward into a gray sky spotted with occasional puffs of clouds.

"Thank You, Lord. I shall never forget my promise," I prayed.

My knapsack lay where I had left it. Nearby ground showed signs of visitors. How close they had come, and yet they had missed my belongings—and me. Truly I counted my blessings.

Despite the joy I found in traveling along the waterways of the Allegheny Valley, I decided to return to Longmeadow for a visit. My father's home was still noisy with the shouts and cries of young children. But it was still delightful being with my own Chapman clan. When I planned my return to Pennsylvania, I persuaded Nathaniel to come along. He no longer had to stretch his frame to appear taller. He was almost as tall as I was, but his feet were soft and tender.

"My best traveling time is made when the ground is cold and my feet are bare," I told him. "An icy earth quickens one's step faster than anything."

His eyes widened in disbelief. "But don't your toes freeze off?" he asked.

"Never!" I replied. "I still have all six I started out with."

Nat's jawbone dropped to the floor. "Six!" he yelped. "I have ten toes. You mean you've lost four of your—'' He stopped, catching my joking smile, and he knew I was teasing.

Returning to Pennsylvania, I decided it would be well if Nathaniel and I built a cabin. For myself, such a permanent settlement was unnecessary. Whenever I stayed anywhere for any length of time, the urge to travel took over. I had to be on my way, discovering new paths, meeting new people.

But Nathaniel was different. True enough, Nathaniel took pleasure in different lands and places. Yet he also liked having a place to call home. Respecting his wishes, we exchanged two weeks of labor with a Pennsylvania farmer for an old shed he had on his property. We rebuilt the shed into a sturdy cabin. The earthen floor gave me the feeling of still being outside, while the wooden walls provided a homelike shelter.

The trading post at nearby Franklin offered us supplies and conversation. News of George Washington's death saddened us, but an awareness that John Adams and Thomas Jefferson were in command gave us a sense of security.

The beginning of a new century gave cause for excitement. Nathaniel and I celebrated with a hearty helping of rabbit stew and cornmeal.

Nathaniel hoisted a cup of steaming apple cider high in the air. ''Here's to a wonderful 1800!'' my brother exclaimed. ''May good fate and fortune follow you everywhere!''

''Same to you!'' I answered. ''And may the faith of the Lord grow ever stronger and lead your way.''

Somehow our wishes did not ring true. Nathaniel soon became ill. I stayed with him constantly, seldom stepping outside. Hot broth and a warm fire helped. But I knew I would have to go for supplies and I hated to leave him.

Packing a small knapsack, I set out for the Allegheny River. We had a small canoe hidden near the shore. I was glad to find that it rested where we had left it.

The ice was running. No sooner had I shoved the canoe into the flow than ugly chunks of ice hit against it. My canoe tipped and turned, bobbing in the water like an apple in a dunking party.

I fought the currents as best I could. Suddenly I spotted a giant piece of ice floating nearby. Quickly I guided the canoe toward the icecake, scrambled onto it, and lifted my vessel onto the ice.

The chunk of ice rolled rapidly through the currents, neatly pushing aside other chunks. I lay down in my own canoe, snuggled up, and proceeded to fall asleep. Staying up with my brother had offered little chance for rest.

For hours my frozen vessel rolled along the river.

Nothing disturbed my slumber. When I finally awakened, I knew I had passed my point of destination. As rapidly as I could, I shoved my canoe into the water and paddled ashore. Firmly tying my vessel, I hurried to the trading post.

Once I had the needed supplies, I set out on foot to return to the cabin. The currents were flowing too quickly downstream and I would have made no progress at all. The land was firm and hard.

"Beware of the wolves, Johnny," the storeowner warned me, waving goodbye. "They grow more than a mite hungry in this cold."

"I'll remember," I said, nodding. "I'm not ready to become a meal for any varmints of the woods."

I headed back, following the paths and trails I knew well. I kept an open eye for the fresh footprints of wild creatures among the woods. Whenever it looked as if I might meet up with a band of wolves, I skirted the area.

I pushed myself forward, walking every hour there was light. Some nights the moonlight reflected the bright crusts of snow and I could see clearly enough to travel. Disgusted songs came from the owls, angry at the intrusion of a human being in the nighttime kingdoms.

"I wish you no harm," I called back. "You may tend your forest in peace."

Finally, our cabin appeared in the distance. I hastened ahead, eager to greet Nathaniel's cheerful face. But as I neared our doorway, I saw that the snow had been disturbed. Someone was in the cabin besides my brother. Sounds from inside reached my ears. They were clearly the chants of Indians. I dashed forward, uncertain as to what I would find and realizing that great danger might await me.

As I flung open the wooden door, my gaze met the eyes of four Indian braves standing above my brother's bed.

Planting God's Seeds

My mouth fell open but no words came out. As I glanced down at my brother, I saw that his nightshirt was spread open and his chest glistened with sweat.

"Nate," I blurted, "are you all right?"

No answer came. My brother's eyes were closed and I could not see any movement. I dropped beside the bed, wondering if my younger brother still lived.

"Nate?" I repeated. "Can you hear me?"

This time I saw a slight movement of my brother's eyelids. I sighed in relief. At least he was still alive.

"Sick. Bad spirits."

I turned, focusing on the Indian who had spoken. He did not meet my look, gazing instead at my brother.

"Sick. We shout away bad spirits."

So, that is what the sounds were when I was outside. I had feared some wild human beasts were attacking my brother. Instead, the Indians were trying to help.

Feeling heat upon my hand, I stared at the quilt

that covered my brother. He was taking my hand, feebly trying to share some message with me. I felt a gentle squeeze and noticed that Nathaniel's lips were trembling. He was trying desperately to speak.

"Nate, it's Johnny," I offered. "I've come back with supplies. You'll be well soon. I'll take care of you now."

With all the strength he could muster, Nathaniel attempted to smile. I gripped his hot hand, hoping to pass my own strength to him.

"You'll be well soon, Nate. The good Lord has little need for you now, not as much as I do anyway."

Sounds behind me captured my attention. The Indians were leaving. I rose to my feet.

"Please, please, stay with me for a while," I suggested. "I have fresh supplies."

It was clear that not all of my guests understood my words. Three of the Indian visitors looked at the fourth, the man who had spoken earlier. He was their leader. What he decided would be their course of action.

"Not good you leave sick man," the leader said to me. "Why you not stay with him?"

"I couldn't. I had to go to the trading post to get supplies. We had to have food."

It was impossible to know if my words carried any value. All four of the men simply looked at each other and then back at me.

"Bad spirits here. Make man sick."

I gazed back at Nathaniel. "No, bad weather make man sick, not bad spirits."

The leader of the Indians nodded. I was not certain he understood, but he seemed friendly enough. Remembering the band of Indians who had chased me earlier, I gave thanks for the kinder visitors in the cabin.

"Stay and eat with me," I invited. "Surely you would enjoy a warm meal before going outside into the cold."

Thus it was decided. The Indians shared a meal with me. They devoured the deer meat eagerly, savoring the hardtack and stewed herbs. I learned the Indian leader had befriended a pair of Vermont trappers who had settled in Pennsylvania. Now and then the other three Indians recognized words the two of us shared. Their eyes sparkled and they nodded with happy smiles.

Our meal completed, we retired to the warmth of the hearth. Flames in the wooden pile crackling in the fireplace brightened the room. Feeling at ease, the Indians began singing a few of their tribal chants. I sat on Nathaniel's bed, holding his hand. He looked up at me and smiled. It was clear he enjoyed the company.

"We chant away evil spirits," the Indian leader declared, his friends surrounding the bed. "Make sick man well."

I was about to argue. I knew the Indians of the territory had many gods whom they worshiped. Somehow it did not seem right, calling upon all these false idols to heal my brother.

And yet, these were men—strangers—who were willing to share the best way they knew to help Nathaniel. Was it truly the time to start arguing with them? No, this would not be the way of my own beloved Savior. I recalled Proverbs 27:10: "Better is a neighbour that is near than a brother far off." These men were my neighbors here in the wilderness. Surely, prayer was prayer in whatever form. I felt a special love for my guests, these so-called savages who stood praying for a stranger.

I listened to the chants and singing. The words were

strange to me, and they continued for a long time. Yet I waited.

And when they had finished, I brought out the Bible, the worn old book that Nathaniel and I knew so well. I began to read from it. The Indians sat silently, their eyes intent upon me. Perhaps the words were new, their thoughts unclear, but the messages seemed to comfort and soothe the Indians.

Or maybe it was because I had listened to the Indians with patience. It took time to win friends, I decided.

"The voice of God speaks to all men," I told the Indian leader. "His words are in this Book. He loves us all and He is the one who answers prayers."

I wondered if my new friend understood. Finally, he took my hand in his.

"Friends," he said. "Friends."

I smiled and nodded. "Yes, friends."

Within an hour they were gone. As I cleared away the wooden plates and bowls, I felt good inside. Nathaniel's spirits were lifted, and the supplies of food had replenished him. I threw a few more logs on the fire, then settled in for sleep.

"Thank You, my Lord and Master, for a day well spent," I prayed.

By morning Nathaniel seemed to have improved even more. In a few more days, he was back to full strength. Once more, the Lord had proven His kindness and mercy.

In return for the Lord's blessings, I felt a new joy in planting, a desire to refurnish the soil with the goodness He had shared. I worked for various settlers, gathering seeds from their apple orchards. Then I planted my own seedlings, and eagerly awaited the fresh green of infant buds and hearty sprouts. Passing travelers often stopped to purchase my wares. It

gave me joy knowing that the richness of the Lord
would thus be carried into new lands.

Nathaniel grew weary of staying in one place. I
knew the feeling myself, so I understood when he told
me he was off to discover new lands west.

"There's much talk of good land in Ohio,"
Nathaniel said. "Are you certain you wouldn't like
to come with me?"

I looked around at the sea of young apple trees
breaking through the rich topsoil. Yes, it would be
exciting to pick up stakes and travel new paths again.
But what of these young sprouts? Who would care for
them?

"No, Nate. I have children here to take care of,"
I answered. "There is much here to do."

News that Father and Lucy would soon be coming
west brought joy to both Nathaniel and me. Surely
the state of Massachusetts would be a mite more quiet
with the Chapman clan leaving it.

It was not my wish to become a borrower. Yet my
desire to raise nurseries and orchards of apple trees
grew too strong to control. I signed two promissory
notes, pledging to repay the two one-hundred dollar
loans in either land or apple trees.

Although I still considered myself a wanderer, the
lands near Franklin, Pennsylvania, came to be
something of a home to me. I knew every curve and
ripple of French Creek.

My system for planting appleseeds was pure and
simple. First I'd find a spot where I knew the land
was good for planting and growing. The cider mills
in Allegheny County provided me with seeds when
I washed out the pomace left over after the apples were
pressed. I carried the seeds in a bag on my shoulder,
planting them at the proper time and enclosing the

spot with a brush fence. From then on, I paid close attention to rid the area of weeds and rocks.

"Johnny, have you titles to the land you're planting?" one neighbor asked me once.

"No," I answered. "I don't want to own the land, just make it a mite richer for use than before I came."

"But you could have wealth. Your hands raise fine plants into sturdy trees. It is a gift from God."

I smiled. "I would like to think that. But I also hold much faith in Proverbs 11:28: 'He that trusteth in his riches shall fall.' If God has given me the gift to make things grow within his soil, I shall use that gift for His glory. I believe a man who works for the glory of the Lord in this world shall enjoy the glory of heaven in the next."

There were those who understood my thinking. But many of my neighbors did not. They turned away, shaking their heads, wondering how such peculiar notions planted themselves in my head. It did not bother me. One cannot live according to the thoughts of another person. One must live according to God's rules and directions.

Apples! What more beautiful sight could there be than a rich, full apple in the warm rays of an afternoon sun. Full of good healthy juices. Ready to be plucked and chawed by man and child alike. Ready to be cut and dried in autumn, strung and hung from ceiling rafters until needed for sauces in the winter. Apple butter. Is there any better taste? What better smell than apples being cooked in giant brass kettles during the summertime so that apple butter preserves might be shared months later? Yes, apples were truly God's glorious gift to his hungry multitudes.

"You would have us wonder why God did not include apples with the fish and loaves of bread when the disciples fed the hungry people at Gennesareth," one traveling preacher told me when I shared my feelings with him one evening.

I laughed. But I could not help but think a bit of apple butter on the bread might have turned that meal into a grand feast!

And if apples could not be eaten at once or stored away for future consumption, they could be bartered. No trading establishment would turn away a bushel of apples. Eggs, deer skin, beaver pelts, live hens— all could be bartered for fresh apples. Better than money in the pocket.

Not to forget the delicious cider that might be gleaned from a collection of ripe, fresh apples. Even the poorer quality fruits could become liquid gold, ready to tickle and delight any dry throat.

Although my apples satisfied most of my needs, I must confess to enjoying a few more pleasures. A friendly cow I called Dorie provided rich milk and cream on a regular basis, while beehives filled my back yard. My meager cabin soon found itself surrounded by other cabins. When neighbors dropped by for visiting, I offered them honey from my hives, milk from Dorie, and apples from my orchards.

"You have all a man could want," one friend observed, "without even having to leave your home."

True enough, I thought. But there was something else this particular man began to crave. I began to feel too settled in, too much at home in Pennsylvania. Could I not be more useful elsewhere? America was growing, and I was standing still. People spoke of heading west, of pioneering new lands. Ohio. More and more folks were heading to Ohio. Were there apple trees in Ohio? There should be, I was sure.

Stuffing as many seeds into leather bags as I could, I sold my worldly goods, bought a horse, and headed into the Southwest. It was a new adventure, and I must admit to a bit of fear and trembling inside of me.

Yet, alone as I was, I did not feel alone.

"As long as You are with me, Lord, I shall never be alone," I prayed into the brisk breezes. "Guard and protect me."

5

On to Ohio

Following the Allegheny River was like accompanying an old friend. People who have never known a river well have missed a good friend. How often I thought back on my childhood days, growing up along the smooth flowing Connecticut waters. Then it was the Allegheny, offering swiftly flowing currents for canoeing and rafting.

Now I traveled west to Beaver Creek and on to the wide waters of the Ohio River. Few settlers called the lands home. Indian fights were still too frequent and bloody. Border scouts patrolled the area, trying to maintain the Greenville Treaty of 1795 which outlawed fighting between white man and Indian.

But it was good soil for apples, that much was clear. At Marietta, the Ohio Company had set up a Donation Tract to encourage settlers. The company had ruled that to gain one hundred acres, a settler had to plant no fewer than fifty apple trees and twenty peach trees within three years. The only trouble was that appleseed and bud sprouts were few. Though land was cheap and orchards easy to tend once they were started, getting the seeds was a challenge.

Challenge? I welcomed it. Often I read 22:29 in Proverbs: "Seest thou a man diligent in his business? he shall stand before kings; he shall not stand before mean men."

My journey took me to a tiny village in the Muskingam Valley. A tavern, trading establishments, and several cabins rested peacefully in the midst of Indian country. A man named Ebenezer Zane and his men had settled the land, and the village was thus labeled Zanesville. As I rode my horse up to the tavern, a tall fellow with ample beard and leathery skin approached my horse and extended a friendly hand.

"Welcome to Zanesville, Ohio, stranger. Those packing bags you're carrying look ready to explode." I dismounted, watching my hospitable friend scratch under his whiskers. "My name is John Larabee. Got a peck of gold you're carrying?"

"And mine is John Chapman," I answered. "No, the bags have no gold to most people, but it's nature's gold to me. Appleseeds they are, ready to find a new home and soak up fresh sun and rain. Ready to burst into bloom with blossoms a-plenty. Ready to provide the best nourishment God has to offer for men's bodies."

John Larabee still scratched his beard as he walked around my horse. "You have quite a tongue in that mouth of yours, Mister Chapman. I'm one who enjoys sharin' talk. Do you plan to settle around here?"

"For a while, I guess," I said. "If the soil is good for growing apple trees, it's good enough for me to spend some time."

"Where did you get the seeds?"

"From the finest cider presses in western Pennsylvania," I replied.

"Hm-m. Well, a fellow by the name of Isaac Stadden just moved in along the Licking River. Word is
that he and his wife come over from Northumberland
County in Pennsylvania. I imagine you'd be feeling
right at home in these parts."

I nodded. If all were as friendly as John Larabee,
Zanesville might be a right good place to spend some
time.

By nightfall, I found myself sharing a meal of roast
duck with Larabee. It was not the usual pioneer cabin,
that was certain. With time and care, Larabee had
built himself a tiny home within a huge, hollow
sycamore tree. In truth, I felt myself a bit cramped,
but I would never have let my gracious host know.
He was proud of his home.

"It keeps out the rain and night varmints," Larabee
said proudly.

Indeed it did. And on that night we shared, his
house of bark heard many wild tales. John had served
in the Revolutionary War, just like my pa, and
Larabee's tales of General Washington, General
Knox, and General "Mad" Anthony Wayne held me
silent for as long as I can recall.

"Old Henry Knox sat on his horse like a moun-
tain on a pony," Larabee said. "The fellow weighed
about four hundred pounds, I believe, and he knew
more about guns than anyone."

"I'm hoping the gentleman was given a fresh horse
each day," I offered. "For the horse's sake, if no
other."

Larabee laughed. "They should have, that's truth
indeed. Whenever we saw anything big, we got to
sayin' 'it's as big as a Knox!' "

"So that's it," I exclaimed. "My pa always said

that back in Connecticut. But we always thought he was saying, 'It's as big as an ox!' We just didn't listen close enough.''

''If your pa was in the Revolution, he knew about our good General Knox. You just didn't listen close.''

Yes, I liked this John Larabee. When he finished his stories about the Revolution, he went on talking about the Indians of the territory. I shared my own meager experiences, but they did not hold a shadow to Larabee's. The blazing fire we sat around outside the sycamore dwindled into tiny ashes and sparks while we talked. Only the owls hooting broke the silence of the night. By morning, I had decided to spend some time in the region.

''If you help me clear a few acres and plant some corn, I'll help you with your apple tree planting.''

''A worthy exchange,'' I told Larabee.

The soil looked rich for growing just about anything that might be put into it. I was certain the appleseeds I had brought along would flourish in their new surroundings. When I went to visit Isaac Stadden, he gave me permission to plant seedlings on his farm. I thanked him kindly.

Once my seedlings were planted, I tended them carefully. Larabee chuckled at my fussing, calling me an ''old mother hen with her chicks.''

I did not mind the teasing. In a sense, the bright buds that appeared in the darkened soil were like new babes. They had to be protected from weeds, as babes have to be protected from temptation and sin. They had to be fed and nourished by the sun and the rain God provided. If tended properly, the apple trees would bear rich fruit much like a man or woman serves the cause of goodness. Yes, perhaps the seeds were my children. I promised to do all I could to be a good father.

But sometimes trouble comes from unseen sources. Having stayed in the territory called Licking Bottoms for some time, I watched my trees grow from babes to mighty giants, their branches laden with fresh fruit. I was picking apples in my orchard one afternoon when I heard horsehoofs in the distance. Cupping my hand over my eyes, I stretched to see who might be scurrying along the trail so rapidly.

It was a woman. I recognized her as being Mrs. Isaac Stadden. By the time she halted her carriage, I stood beside the dusty road.

"I'll get some water for your horse," I offered. "Perhaps you might be a mite thirsty yourself."

For the first time I caught a glimpse of Mrs. Stadden's face. Her cheeks were flushed, and her eyes blazed. It was soon clear that Mrs. Isaac Stadden did not make this trip out of friendly spirit.

"Mr. Chapman, or do you answer to the name of Appleseed John?" Mrs. Stadden gripped the handle of her horsewhip.

There was anger, simple and clear, in the woman's voice. Whatever offense she felt I had done was major.

"John Chapman is my name," I answered respectfully, "the name given me by my father and mother. Folks here and there have labeled me the other, but I have no use for it myself."

"I would think not!" Mrs. Stadden snapped. "Mr. Chapman, there are those who would understand that you were the first to plant these appleseeds in this valley. I want you and everyone else to understand that *I* was the one who carried appleseeds from my own former home in Pennsylvania. You were not the first to do so!"

I shook my head. "I never made such a claim. I have no wish to be known as the first of anything. I carry appleseeds with me in the hope I'll find good soil for them. If you do so too, then perhaps we might enjoy a partnership carrying the fruits of God to the bodies of men.''

Mrs. Stadden's expression did not change. If anything, she seemed to stiffen even further in the seat of her carriage.

"You have strange notions, Mr. Chapman. I am always somewhat suspicious of a man who dresses like a scarecrow in the farm field. Some people say they have never seen you with shoes upon your feet. You speak of God, but you like heathen Indians. Folks say you bathe in the river, when you do bathe that is. Yes, you are a mighty peculiar person.''

"Everything you say is true enough," I answered, glancing down at my bare feet. "Frankly though, I hadn't thought that people paid so much mind to me.''

The woman began pounding the handle of her whip into the palm of her hand. "One as strange as you are can hardly go unnoticed.''

"Well, as for myself, I only hope I might be allowed to do my planting and praying as I wish, doing no harm to anyone. I apologize for whatever misunderstanding I've caused, if I've contributed.''

Mrs. Stadden directed her horses around, displaying poise and skill in her carriage. But before she left, she shot me one more angry look.

"You are every bit as peculiar as I thought you might be," she offered, "but from the looks of your orchard, you do indeed know how to raise apple trees. I can understand why you are known as Appleseed John. And I confess to being a bit jealous of your reputation.''

"We are only God's servants, Mrs. Stadden. Without Him and His blessings, we could grow nothing.''

The woman said no more. She looked confused.

Maybe she had expected more of a fight from me.
Clearly she had been hurt by someone's words. How
cruel people can be, often without realizing the pain
their words bring. Mrs. Stadden must have taken
great pride in her planting. She felt she had brought
something special to the wilderness. It was a pride I
felt myself.

But one must be careful to hold pride in its place
or it may become vanity and conceit. I recalled the
words of I Samuel 2:3: "Talk no more so exceeding
proudly; let not arrogancy come out of your mouth:
for the Lord is a God of knowledge, and by him
actions are weighed."

I stood beside the path, watching the carriage disap-
pear into the distance.

Returning to my work, I promised that I would
soon call upon Mrs. Stadden. Perhaps she might show
me the trees she had planted. There was so much to
learn about the richness of this Ohio valley. If I shared
my knowledge of the soil and plants with her, she
might be willing to share with me. Was this not what
our Savior intended for His world?

6

Beginnings and Endings

I enjoyed visiting with families as I traveled. It was always a pleasure to share good food and conversation with new friends. I had little fear that Mrs. Isaac Stadden and I would reach a better understanding. Call me a fool for such a notion.

When I visited her home and rode through the paths of bountiful orchards, I could hardly believe my eyes. Every apple tree boasted branches of rich, full fruit.

"God has picked you as a special servant!" I exclaimed. "He has sent you many fine blessings."

"I bought the land and had the seeds planted," Mrs. Stadden declared, jerking the reins she held. "My hired workers have cared for the saplings and the trees. I am no one's servant."

"We are all servants of God," I answered. "He provides us with the seeds and that is the beginning. Without the seeds, there would be nothing."

We dismounted and led our horses through a sunlit

row of trees. I prayed for a way that Mrs. Stadden and I could be friends. But she would have none of it.

"You are strange, Mr. Chapman," the woman said. "What kind of man moves from place to place, planting seeds and growing trees? You have no wife, no children, no real home. Surely you must be lonely?"

"Lonely? No, I can't say as I am, Mrs. Stadden. The Lord is always with me. He is my constant companion."

The answer did not suit my friend. "That all sounds well and good, Mr. Chapman, but you are too much a vagrant for my understanding. You are too different."

I gazed around at the trees we were admiring. "Each one of these creations is an apple tree. Yet no tree has the same leaves or the same number of fruit on the same branches. Is one tree better than another because its branches are shaped differently? I don't think so.''

"But a person is not a tree or an apple," Mrs. Stadden said.

"We are all creations of God," I answered. "I believe He loves us for our differences as well as our similarities.''

We talked for over an hour that afternoon, yet I am not certain we understood each other any better when we were finished. I left Mrs. Stadden, knowing that she was a proud woman. I'm afraid she thought I was somewhat of a fool.

No matter. One cannot please everyone. I vowed to remember Mrs. Stadden as I prayed. Surely her gift with growing riches in the Lord's earth was considerable. I still felt she was a special servant.

One morning, as I planted a fresh supply of seeds which I had gathered on a recent trip to Pennsylvania, I gazed up to discover a covered wagon approaching. The sight was not uncommon along Owl Creek in north central Ohio. But the driver looked familiar. I dropped the bag of seeds I held and raced forward.

"Pa!" I shouted so loud the whole Ohio countryside could hear me. "Pa!"

How long we stood hugging each other I do not recall. I *do* remember that the warmth fought off the late winter breezes.

Through the day and night, stories flowed. I rejoiced at learning about the folks back in Longmeadow. Pa could not get enough of my own wild tales of Pennsylvania and Ohio. How quickly the years passed before us as we swapped memories.

And yet the years were clearly etched on the leathery skin of my father's face. The wrinkles were deep, the eyes weary. Lucy had lost her youthful glow as well. Having borne ten children in twenty-two years, it is

no wonder the years had taken their toll on the bright face of her youth. One more babe she cradled in her arms, one of the six my father and stepmother had brought west.

"Finding you was easy enough," my father said. "People told us often of the Apple John who travels the land planting seeds."

"So it's Apple John, is it?" I asked.

Lucy smiled.

"I've heard you called Johnny Appleseed," she murmured. "It is spoken with much respect, I believe."

"I hope so," I answered. "If by accident someone knows my Chapman label, I'd not want to bring embarassment to the family name."

"You never have," Pa whispered, "and I know you never will."

It brought me a special joy having the Chapman clan close by. I helped them settle near Duck Creek above Marietta. But in 1807, Pa's health began to fail.

One night, as I sat beside his bed, I felt his hand take mine. His breathing was slow and heavy.

"Are you there, Johnny-boy?" he asked.

"I am here, Pa. Right beside you."

His hand gripped mine more tightly. Yet the old strength was sapped by the years.

"Johnny, do you remember long ago when you dreamed of that mystery lady?"

"Yes, Pa. I remember."

"Well, boy, I've been dreaming of her, too. She's been motioning me to come to her. I—I think I'm about ready to go."

I sat silent for several moments, feeling tears burn my cheeks. Memories filled my mind. The stories of the Revolutionary War, of General Washington, of the days back in Longmeadow.

And as my father's life slipped away, I stroked his hand.

"Take him to You, O Lord," I prayed. "Have mercy on him and give him peace."

As I stood beside my father's grave days later, I knew a door was closing on my life. Yet I could not help but remember the death of Jesus and His resurrection. Through His death He gave us life. With this in mind, I planted seeds as I had never planted before. Each time, I thought of my father. In a way, I felt my father was now enjoying a new life, and this new life that I was planting into God's earth would be his memorial.

Certain that my father now shared heavenly life with the Lord, I promised to carry the Bible and the Lord's Word to new frontiersmen and their families. I sent away for pamphlets and papers I could carry westward to give people I visited.

Once Lucy and my family were taken care of, I grew eager to move on. Orchards in the area were already flourishing. Surely there were new lands farther west that were empty.

But dark times lay ahead.

Indians on the Warpath

Although there had been no major open fighting between the white man and the Indian, no one could say there were peaceful feelings in many places. When other Indian chiefs had gathered to sign a peace treaty back in 1795, the powerful leader Tecumseh was not among them. As I traveled from place to place and talked to people at their settlements, I felt much uneasiness.

"I've heard the Shawnee Prophet, brother of the mighty Tecumseh, thinks he is a god," one settler told me. "He claims to have dreams revealing a new future for the Indian."

Another settler added to the story.

"More and more tribal leaders have been coming to meetings along the St. Marys and the Auglaize Rivers. Shawnee Prophet talks to them. Senecas, Ottawas, Wyandots—leaders of many tribes have come. There's trouble ahead, I'm certain."

The stories worried me. As I roamed across the wilderness, I looked at the wide spaces, the open lands. God had provided so much land. Why could people not live in peace?

By late 1807, signs of trouble grew even stronger. Drums from Indian tribes pounded out mysterious warnings. Scouts carried secret dispatches. Tribal councils sent strange messages through smoke into the blue sky.

A year later the Shawnee Prophet and Tecumseh moved to the Tippecanoe branch of the Wabash River in northwestern Indiana. Other tribes followed them.

White men fanned the flames of discontent. One day, as I stopped at a settlement store, the shopkeeper kept up a lively conversation from the moment I entered.

"Always glad to serve the famous Apple John, yes I am," he declared. "I hear tell you can turn the hardest rock soil into a blooming orchard. Heard tell a fellow almost drowned when he bit into one of your apples and the juice flowed out."

I chuckled. It wasn't the first time I'd heard such wild tales. The storekeeper seemed a friendly fellow—that is, until two Indians came in. The mood changed quickly. Immediately the storekeeper's face paled, his manner stiffened. Moving directly behind the cash register, he did not take his stare off the visitors.

The two Indians sensed the atmosphere. They whispered quietly to themselves, selected a few articles from the shelves, and approached the counter.

"Sorry, we don't serve your kind," the storekeeper snapped.

The Indians stood puzzled. They held out their money, not quite understanding the situation.

"We-we pay," one of the visitors mumbled.

"Not here you don't," the storekeeper answered,

removing the goods from the counter. "I suggest you be on your way. There's another store down the river about four miles. The fellow there isn't particular about who he sells to."

I watched the two Indians. Their faces wore shame and disappointment. Silently they retreated out of the store.

The air seemed suddenly stifling. Without saying anything, I began retracing my steps. I put the goods I was holding back onto their shelves.

"Say, Apple John, what are you doing there?" the storekeeper asked.

"Changed my mind about trading here," I replied.

"Why's that?"

"Well, as far as I could see, I have some of the same money as those two fellows. If they can't buy anything with their money, how can I?"

The storekeeper smiled. "You don't understand,

friend. Those Indians are no good. They're shiftless and sneaky. I don't need their business.''

I shook my head. ''They did not treat you unkindly, as I see it. They came to buy a few goods and were willing to pay. You do not choose to trade with them and I do not choose to trade with you.''

''But—but they're Indians!''

''So they are,'' I answered, stepping to the door. ''They are also creatures of God, just like the two of us. God does not judge us by the color of our skin. And we shouldn't either. Now, I must be gone. Four miles is not a long distance to travel alone, but I think it might be more enjoyable with two companions.''

I hurried away, leaving the storekeeper looking puzzled. The two Indians welcomed my company and by the time we parted hours later, we had become good friends.

But if the two Indians I encountered that day were friendly, many more in the territory were not. The Great Prophet and Tecumseh succeeded in stirring up many of their tribal allies. They felt a bitterness against the American settlers who were traveling west to build their homes and futures. British leaders, still angry about the Revolutionary War days, did not help matters any. They fed guns and ammunition to the Indians, often providing trained soldiers to lead attacks. They must have hoped they could win the United States back to British rule.

I continued my wanderings and my plantings. It was a good feeling to be welcomed into cabins by friendly settlers. ''Johnny Appleseed, come tell us the news,'' a cheerful voice would ring out as I approached. Over simmering stew and biscuits, I brought each family stories of all I had seen and heard.

Happier still I was to bring them the word of God.

I urged people to live in the reflection of their God and Creator.

"You are truly a holy messenger," one woman told me. "We shall remember the day John Chapman graced our doorway."

Those were welcome words. They were words that gave me courage to brave the wilderness and continue my planting.

I seldom traveled at night. Daytime was safer. But one evening as I entered the edge of a heavy woodland, I heard strange drums. The light of a campfire drew me closer. With trees cloaking my presence, I watched and listened.

Near a crackling fire stood a British trader I had met here and there during my travels. He rode from village to village carrying a wagon loaded with kitchen pans and farm tools. But on this night, he was trading the devil's goods. With flashing eyes and strong voice, he demonstrated two different kinds of rifles. The Indians who sat nearby were clearly fascinated. I could not tell if each one understood his words, but they did not take their eyes from him as he showed how to hold the guns and fire them.

"The British stand ready to assist you in every way," the trader promised. "Guns and ammunition are all yours. The best way of proving their worth is to use them."

I trembled. Did the British not know what they were doing? Bloodshed answered nothing. Clearly the trader was doing all he could to stir up trouble.

"Willow Springs might be the best place to test your new weapons," the trader declared.

Willow Springs. A small settlement just five miles away. Once more I shivered, imagining men, women, and children falling in a surprise attack. They would

not even have time to flee to a block house. It would be a massacre, a bloody slaughter.

"We've got work to do, Sally," I told my mule. "Let's travel—and travel fast."

Good old Sally sensed the urgency of our mission. She'd been traveling all day long, but she seemed to know how important time was.

The village of Willow Springs slept peacefully in the moonlight. Only a few firelights brightened the darkness with an occasional owl lending voice to the stillness. But the Lord had given me a mission, and I set about it eagerly.

"The Spirit of the Lord brings me here," I shouted, pounding on each cabin door. "I blow the trumpet of warning in the wilderness and spread the alarm. Enemy tribes approach. They bring death and a devouring flame."

Weary men rubbed their eyes in disbelief. Women and children exchanged worried looks, the candles they held heightening their fearful faces.

"Who are you to tell us this?" one bearded gentleman asked. Suspicion edged his tone.

"I am John Chapman, perhaps better known to you as Apple John or Johnny Appleseed. I suggest you take your family to the nearest block house for shelter and safety. Dawn is approaching and the Indians will attack with the rising sun."

My message was heeded. The folks of Willow Springs filled their wagons hastily. The Indians would find no blood to shed in the settlement of Willow Springs.

But many folks were not as fortunate as those of Willow Springs. All too often I came upon a lone pioneer who had fallen victim to a band of roaming savages. Within a humble grave I laid many a fallen stranger.

"Those that be planted in the house of the Lord shall flourish in the courts of our God." The words of Psalm 92:13 seemed appropriate. Carefully I pressed a sturdy wooden cross above each grave.

Traveling alone became too dangerous. I took refuge with Caleb Palmer and his family near the west branch of the Huron River. News reached us that war with England and the renegade Indians was declared in June of 1812. It saddened me to think once again our world was thrown into conflict, a turmoil I remembered hearing about when just a child.

Knowing my traveling nature, our neighbors asked me to bring them news as I made my way along the river and onto Lake Huron. I agreed, hoping that my actions might help save lives.

"Good to have you on our side," one man told me.

I shook my head. "I am not taking sides," I answered, "except to be on the side of the Lord. Man has no right to kill another man, whatever color he might be."

"But those redskins are savages. You've seen what they've done to our white people."

"I have seen slaughtered Indians, too. No, it is not the color of a person's skin that makes the difference. It is what lives beneath that skin. Killing is the devil's tool. I will be a scout to save lives, nothing more. I will share news as I see it. But I'll not lift a weapon to take any lives."

"You are a fair man, John Chapman. Surely the Lord guards whatever path you follow."

That path almost brought me to an early end.

One day Caleb Palmer and I were working in a field. Indians were said to be in the territory and if we spotted any, we were to fire a shot in the air. Guns were to be fired for no other reason.

Suddenly a shot rang out. It came from a cabin

belonging to a farmer named Woodcock. Another shot
followed, then another. As fast as squirrels skittering
up a tree, Caleb and I raced to our barn and jumped
on our horses. Neither Caleb nor I was ready to lose
our scalps to Indians.

But as I rode along with Caleb, a curiosity bug bit
me. "I'm goin' back," I shouted to my friend. "Wait
here until I return."

Caleb put up no argument. All he wanted was to
be a safe distance from those Indians.

Returning to our cabin, I threw on some Indian
garb. If spotted by the invaders, I wanted to appear
friendly. They might shoot a white man farmer before
asking any questions.

Slowly and carefully I inspected the land around
Woodcock's farm. Nothing seemed out of the
ordinary. I tied my horse and made my way by foot

around the bushes and trees near the Woodcock buildings. Still no sign of activity.

"Hold your step!" a voice bellowed from the tool shed.

My first urge was to turn and run. But the sun caught the metal of a rifle and I suspected any move I made in retreat would be my last.

From behind the shed stepped a man. I squinted in the sunlight. Why, it was Woodcock! I sprang forward, eager to greet our neighbor, whom we supposed might be dead.

"Stay where you are, redskin!" the man ordered.

"No, no! It's John Chapman from the next farm. I live there with Caleb Palmer. We thought you were dead when we heard shots."

Woodcock lowered his rifle. His face turned into a wide smile. "No, there are no Indians. But a mighty fine deer just paid a final visit to this farm. Haven't had meat in weeks."

"You mean it was you who shot?" I asked. "Don't you know you are only supposed to shoot in case of attack?"

Woodcock looked down at his feet. "When a man's got a wife and kids to feed, he sometimes forgets such rules. I'm sorry if my shootin' caused anyone trouble. But I've got a beautiful buck ready to skin and dress if you're interested."

Relieved that the attack had not been real, I agreed to help Woodcock. By the time I headed back to find Caleb, I had a venison ham hanging from my side.

The hours had drifted by slowly for Caleb. When I returned, he was almost in a state of panic. Once again I had a rifle trained on me before I could identify myself.

"Stop, Caleb! Put your gun down. It's John!"

"Chapman, you old fool cuss. I was about ready

to blow you across Ohio. What's that hanging from your side?''

I glanced down, lifting the meat. "It's a venison ham, fresh from Woodcock's farm. Those were the shots we heard. Just a hungry man hunting a careless deer.''

"You almost had a bullet through you, Johnny boy. That ham looked mighty like a redskin legging. Another second and we'd been planting you among your own appleseeds.''

The thought gave me a brief shiver. Thinking about the day's events made me aware that I had come close to a final judgment. Much as I longed to meet my Maker, I must confess to wanting a few more years on the soil of this earth.

Worry about the Indians increased. No sooner had I gotten a handsome nursery of trees going near Mansfield than trouble reared its head. The local troops of Mansfield escorted a band of renegade Indians away to Mount Vernon and the town was quiet. When merchant Levi Jones went out to visit John Wallace and William Reed, who were clearing a brickyard, a few Indians lay in ambush. Men working nearby brought the word.

"Those redskins shot Jones first,'' one eyewitness reported. "He managed to break away but they caught up with him.''

"What did they do?'' I asked.

"They stabbed him, scalped him, grabbed his hat and handkerchief, gave their animal cry and ran off. They're savages, wild blood-thirsty savages!''

The story of Jones's death spread quickly through Mansfield. When Wallace and Reed did not come home, the worst was expected. Families gathered in the blockhouse. But with the soldiers gone, the people did not feel safe.

"And what of the people nearby?" one woman questioned. "Who will warn them about the Indians?"

"Someone should go to Mount Vernon and bring our men back," another woman suggested. "I know they would come back right away if they knew the danger we faced."

I knew what I had to do. No one knew the landscape better than I. Quickly I hurried to my cabin, saddled my best horse, and was off.

The night was moonlit and cool. The air brushed my face like pellets of spring water, keeping me wide awake and my head clear. I remembered the night at Willow Springs when I had gone on a similar mission. The sounds of my horse thundering across the hillsides echoed in the still September air. At each cabin I reached, I leaped from my horse before we had even stopped. The sight of a barefooted, bareheaded scarecrow scampering up the porch must have frightened many a weak-hearted settler.

"Flee for your lives!" I shouted. "Indians are upris-
ing and coming upon you. Head for safety. Destruc-
tion and death follow me. Save yourselves!"

How many times I carried the warning I do not
know. Through the Ohio forests I raced, carrying
word of possible doom. The settlers reacted quickly,
hurrying to shelter.

By the time I reached Mount Vernon, both horse
and rider were panting. But the job was done. Once
the men from Mansfield heard of the trouble, they
hurried back to their homes. There would be no
Indian attacks that night or the next day.

Wallace and Reed showed up unharmed. Levi
Jones was the only loss. A few days later we learned
that the Indians were not completely without cause
for their actions. They had left rifles as security for
debts at Jones's store. When they came to retrieve
their weapons for money owed, Jones refused to give
them their guns. It helped to explain his murder, but
it still did not excuse it.

Tales of my flight across the countryside followed
me wherever I went. Some of the stories were much
exaggerated. My horse, who had raced through trees
and across trails, disappeared in the retelling of the
tale. It was said I raced in bare feet rather than
bareback, shouting my warnings as I went.

One story from my journey did give me cause for
chuckle. At Fredericktown, one of the residents, a
Samuel Wilson, was so frightened he ran all the way
to the blockhouse, forgetting to put on his pantaloons.
Fortunately he was wearing an overcoat!

But the chuckles were few across the Ohio countryside. There were many stories of bloodshed and
massacre. The tales of families caught completely off
guard left me especially saddened. I increased my

travels, carrying to villages and towns news of any Indian bands I passed.

If the Indians and British hoped to wipe away the American spirit, it was a foolish notion. By the end of 1812, the flames of war drifted into smoke and sparks. Such was the way Caleb Palmer and I found his cabin and crops when we returned after a short trip south.

"Why must this be, John?" my friend asked me. "I hate no man. I ask only to live in peace and to raise food for my family. Now I have lost everything."

"No, Caleb," I answered. "You still have your faith. You still have your family and friends. Above all, you still have God as a partner. He's always by your side, in good times and bad."

Caleb smiled. "You always have the right words at the right time, John. I sometimes forget the things of this world are just that. I'm glad you're around to remind me."

"Let's get the wagon over here, Caleb. We'll clear most of this by nightfall. That will give us an early start in the morning."

With the dawn of a new year, 1813, the fires of war lay in ashes. Peace came to the woodlands and prairie during the year. I was happy to cast away my duties as a trouble scout, hoping I would never again have reason for such actions.

A new page in my life was turning. I was eager to see what it would be.

8

A Rattlesnake Strikes

Planting trees in the spring of 1814 brought me new joy. It had saddened me to know that fresh buds might be trampled by a band of Indians on the warpath or soaked with the blood of some poor dying soul. Yes, peace brought new joy, new life.

It also brought me a wish to change my own life in a small way. Like other settlers, I was a squatter. I enjoyed the freedom of settling on unclaimed land, building a small cabin, and planting a nursery.

But, like my own children—the seeds I planted as the Lord's servant—America was also growing roots. Land was being bought and sold, rented and cultivated. I felt an urge to be a part of this, to share as a landowner a piece of soil in my country.

"You, Johnny?" Caleb exclaimed. "You're too much a drifter. Landowning is for settler folks."

"Now, Caleb, are you trying to tell me I'm not a settler?"

Caleb shook his head. "Johnny, you got somethin' in those feet of yours that starts walking after you've been in any one place a month or two."

"Not true," I argued. "Takes me almost a year to get a good nursery going. That one in Licking Valley took me two. I spent a long time over at Owl Creek, and then there was the nursery on Lake Fork, and the one—"

"All right, Johnny. You win. You do have some settler's blood in that skinny frame of yours. Go ahead and buy your land."

I smiled. "Thanks, good friend. And I just might surprise you and stay on it for good."

On May 31, 1814, a widow lady and I signed a lease with the state of Ohio for 160 acres in Washington Township. Mrs. Jane Cunningham had lost her husband in the Indian fighting, and I was told she needed help. I agreed to turn the land into the finest nursery I could if she would pay the cost of the land. We agreed to build a cabin and, within three years, to clear at least three acres of ground in this quarter section outside Mansfield.

Land owning appealed to me. It offered a sense of obligation. I liked the feeling of having something in my name, legal and proper. I acquired two town lots in Mount Vernon. "I might want to live in town someday," I told Caleb.

My old friend simply shook his head.

More opportunities for land came along. I signed a lease for another spot of land northeast of Mansfield, and six months later acquired 160 acres near the village of Wooster. I could not resist an offer to lease another land parcel on the Black Fork of the old Mohican River.

But enough was enough. Land owning carried responsibility. As I lifted ax and shovel to clear the land, my muscles and bones reminded me I was now in my thirties, no longer a sturdy lad of nineteen.

And still another shaking varmint reminded me that clearing land called for caution.

It was a warm July morning. I had not bothered to build myself a shelter on one of my land parcels near Mansfield. I simply hollowed out a giant log for sleeping. If it rained, I rolled the log over and slept fine underneath it. Just like sleeping in an old canoe and I certainly had done that often enough.

Anyway, I was swinging an ax and enjoying the Lord's golden sun roasting my back. I stopped often to douse myself with creek water. Birds sang nearby, lending some music to my chopping. Even an old owl hooted in the distance, probably thinking it was evening. The woods were so dense he could not know when it was daytime or night.

But one of nature's creatures was not so friendly as the birds who sang their songs. When I raised my ax and crashed it down upon a dead stump, I suddenly heard an angry rattling. It was not an unfamiliar sound.

Quickly I jumped back. Already the rattlesnake leaped out at me. His long slender body was almost hidden against the wood background.

I stood perfectly still, the ax gripped in my hand. My eyes stared into his. He curled slowly into his small rope circle, his rattling never ceasing.

"If you just stand still," an old farmer had told me once, "the rattlesnake is likely to leave you alone."

It soon became clear this snake had never heard the old farmer's advice. I watched its wide head, its tiny eyes peering at me. The rattle at the end of its tail was almost deafening.

"Don't move," I whispered to myself. "Just stand

still.'' Suddenly the creature lunged forward, sinking its mouth into my lower leg.

I felt a sudden heat, a burning flash. Somehow I swung the ax downward. Or perhaps it dropped. However it fell, it caught the clutching reptile and severed its body. Angrily I pulled its head out of my leg, feeling blood and flesh go with it.

Stunned, I fell to the ground. I glanced at the snake's body in its final twitching movements before death. It gave me no sense of victory that I had killed this creature. Yes, it had struck me first. But even within my thinking, I felt saddend.

But there was little time for remorse. My leg felt hot. Gazing down, I saw my pantaloons were covered with blood. Inside I knew the poison was hurrying on its way into other parts of my body.

I stumbled back to my small campsite. I knew what I must do. The ugly snakebite had to be cut away. Every frontiersman knew that.

Grateful for the shade a few nearby oaks provided, I grabbed my cutting knife and dragged myself to the shores of the creek.

The fresh, clear water would help cleanse the wound. I worked as quickly as I could, digging the blade into the torn flesh. The cool water softened the pain, yet I still yelled out.

''Help me, Lord! Give me Your strength!''

The trees echoed my pleas. Once more I heard the songs of my woodland friends. They comforted me, making me feel less alone.

Satisfied the wound was clean, I struggled back to my crude bedsite.

It was not my plan to fall asleep. But how foolish we are to believe our plans make a difference when we are in the Lord's hands. As the brisk breeze swept across the prairie, I felt myself drifting, helplessly floating on some mysterious cloud.

Now and then I felt conscious of the world around me. I could hear the birds singing and I could feel the wind against my skin.

Am I being punished, I wondered. Perhaps the Lord did not look with favor upon me as a landowner. I recalled the old story of Jesus coming to His temple and finding it full of merchants and thieves. He was furious. His father's house desecrated by those seeking money and riches.

My lips moved in quiet prayer. Never did I feel that I was better or above any other man. My desire for land was not from greed. I only wanted to have part of the Lord's good earth and I wanted to feel like a real American.

Minutes became hours, and hours slipped into days. The shade shielded me from the glaring sun. Slowly, ever so slowly, I began to feel stronger. My stomach began to roar like a wild thunderstorm. I knew this was a good sign.

How long I lay at my campsite I do not know. Time was but a blur in my memory.

But much more clear was the Lord and His wishes. As I told Caleb later, I was sure that rattlesnake had been sent as a warning.

"I don't think the Lord finds fault in man holding property," I said. "It's just when a man gets too caught up in the treasures of this world, he forgets the world to come. I fear that's what I did."

"But how do you know that?" asked Caleb.

"I cannot know it in my mind, but I feel it in my heart. The Lord speaks to us in so many ways." I gazed out at the rich field of wheat Caleb was ready to harvest. "Remember not long ago when your farm lay in ruins? Now look at your crops. The Lord tests

our strength and faith. You proved yourself to Him.
I hope I have, too.''

I am not certain that Caleb understood all I said
to him. But I felt sure of myself as I rode away that
afternoon. Little did I know that soon I would be
tested once again.

9

Nature's Nightmare

My rattlesnake story entertained many folks in the weeks and months that followed. Most people had seen prairie and timber rattlers, but few of the settlers had been tested by the mean varmints.

"If you weren't all skin and bones, that rattler wouldn't have laid you up for so long," one store clerk told me. "Got to keep some meat on those bones of yours, Johnny."

There was some truth in his observation. These bones of mine never could keep any flesh on them. More than once I was mistaken for a scarecrow as I roamed across fields. Even a crow flew down once and landed on my shoulder as I surveyed crops.

"If you had a wife to fix regular meals for you, Johnny, you might be fillin' out more." Caleb walked around me as he spoke. "I never did meet a fellow who took less care of himself than you do."

"Sometimes I dream I'm in the next world," I answered my friend. "In the dream, I have two wives.

It makes me think it would suit me better not to have any in *this* world."

I fancy my skinny frame often brought me good results. As I traveled around, staying at the homes of friends and neighbors, I noticed I always got a giant's portion of the food being dished out. I voiced no complaint.

My feelings about owning land changed, largely due to the warning sent by the Lord. I looked for land that other folks didn't want but that would grow a healthy crop of apples. I would plant my seeds, offering them to the glory and goodness of the Creator. What profits I made bought me more seeds, a few pairs of pantaloons, a shirt twice a year, and supplies for my campsite.

By the spring of 1815, I legally held 640 acres of quality land and my two town lots in Mount Vernon. Not bad for a footloose vagabond of forty.

My nurseries now dotted the countryside. I helped train farmers in planting, then moved onto another stretch of empty soil. I knew I was doing the Lord's work. My life had a pattern which revolved around the seasons. Plant seeds, nurture the saplings and watch the trees take hold. How soon beautiful blossoms appeared, bringing quickly the rich juices and glory of fine fruit!

But man must never become too proud of himself, too sure of the work he is doing. It is then the Lord must step in and remind us of His power.

Such was the spring of 1817.

There was no indication anything strange was about to happen. Farmers readied their soil for planting. Seeds of corn, barley, and wheat were slipped within carefully dug holes. By mid-May, the chores of planting were done. All of us awaited the warmth of sunny days and the strength of spring rains.

But 1817 was not to be an ordinary year.

The first sign of trouble probably began when some settler child woke up early in the morning. Glancing out a cabin window, young eyes widened in disbelief.

"Pa! Ma! Come look out the window!" the lad's startled voice woke everyone in the cabin.

"What is it, son?" a weary farmer asked, rubbing his eyes.

"It's winter again!" came the reply.

This time the man moved his son aside and stared out at the fields he had recently sown. Heavy folds of snow rolled on and on. The thick coating covered the countryside.

Silently the farmer's wife moved to her husband's side. She gently slipped her hand inside his to comfort him.

"A snow storm in May?" the farmer mumbled,

still not able to believe his eyes. "It never snows like this so late in the year."

The woman nodded, not saying a word.

Slowly the snow melted, and the Ohio farmers prayed that their seeds, so carefully sown, would not all be washed away. This humble planter prayed too. Hundreds, thousands of apple trees were just getting their start in the world.

What the May snowstorm did not do to the crops, a June frost did. Temperatures plunged well below freezing. The white plague touched the leaves and branches like a deadly disease. Saplings were stripped of their budding greenery, the young fruit killed before having a real chance to live.

The faces of the farmers looked pale and drawn. There were no smiles, no laughter. People stuck to themselves, holing up in their cabins with family. When supplies were needed, bargins were struck between farmer and store owner. Little money changed hands. Notes of I.O.U. were signed on countertops.

I felt little desire to visit the folks I knew. Another mouth to feed was not what anyone needed. So I traveled the Huron and Mohican waters by canoe. I camped by the sites of the Honey and Indian Creeks.

But now and then I journeyed to my orchards, forcing myself to gaze upon the little balls of black waste on the branches. How shriveled they were, how small and ugly. My body shook with hurt and pain. Why, I wondered, why was this happening?

I headed into the forest—rich woodlands that held out the sun and allowed me time for thought. Sturdy oaks stood wide and powerful with evergreen and pine adding color and fragrance. No killer frost could harm their strong structures. I feasted on wild berries and herbs. I listened to the creatures of the night, singing their soothing songs of the darkness.

And I wondered.

The rattlesnake had surely been sent as a warning. Clearly its bite had told me to beware of being caught up in the offerings of this world.

Now, perhaps this was the end. He that controlled everything in the universe, our Creator and Redeemer, might be ready to call me home.

When thinking like this, I was glad that Jesus died for my sins and I was forgiven. Yes, I was ready to share eternal joy with my Maker.

Yet sometimes in the night, I sensed hearing a strange song. The leaves in the trees over my head seemed to be whispering a melody, a song about a man and his children. No, they were not boys and girls, but something else.

Trees, that was it. Hearty full trees with branches weighed down with rich round apples. Yes, it was I in that song—John Chapman—Johnny Appleseed. And it was no farewell tune. It was happy and alive.

Though my body felt tired, my spirit felt light. I felt like running across wide fields and up grassy hillsides. Above me I heard rapping and rustling sounds as rain splattered against the branches.

Suddenly I could keep my eyes open no longer. Sleep fell like a heavy blanket.

When I awoke, I sat up with a start. I rubbed my eyes, but all I could see were foggy outlines of men. I heard their voices and felt them lift me. Then again I slept.

The next time I awakened, I found myself near a crackling fire. This time I could see the figures around me. Indians. Mohicans. I knew by their clothing and I could understand most of their language. One does not live the life of a frontiersman without learning some of the Indian tongue.

"You, Johnny Ap-pleseed?"

The label sounded strange coming from the man who sat next to me. When he spoke, a shiver rushed through me. Could this be a renegade tribe, still carrying vengeance against American settlers?

"Yes, that is a name I am called. My Christian name is John Chapman."

The Indian nodded, and the others seated around the fire nodded with him. The fear left me as quickly as it had come. The faces were friendly and glowing. Anyway, had these people not brought me here from the forest? If they wanted to harm me, they could have done it there.

"You sick. Have fever." The man was clearly the leader of his tribe. "We cool head with pennyroyal and feed you with venison stew."

I remembered none of such things. Now I knew that I had been very sick in the forest. What I thought were dreams were shadows of death.

"Book keep you safe." The chief picked up my Bible and held it so it caught the light of the campfire. "No animal from woods or cave touch you. Footprints of every creature come to you when you sick, but no tooth or claw touch Johnny Appleseed. You good man, it is said, and you carry good book."

I smiled, taking the Bible from the chief's hand. "Thank you for your kindness," I answered. "Would you like me to read from the good Book?"

"Not all know white man's words," the leader answered. "But we will listen if you read."

Carefully I opened the old beaten Bible I carried next to my bosom. For an hour I read, looking up now and then to see the smiles of those around me. Though they may not have understood the words, they

seemed to sense the feelings and love within the pages.

As soon as I was strong enough, I bid my Indian friends goodbye and went back to the Palmer cabin. The Lord had given me a glimpse of death, but it was not yet my time to go. There was more work to be done, more seeds to be sown—into His rich soil and of His loving word. I promised I would do both until my final breath.

Caleb met me at his cabin door with a wild look. He reached out, thinking I was ready to fall.

"What a sight you are!" he exclaimed. "Come in while the wife stirs up a bit of milk and pours honey on some boardcake. You look like you're a-starving."

It was not the kindest greeting I ever received, but Caleb probably spoke the truth. My pantaloons were mudstained and torn, my burlap shirt ragged and stained. Not being able to see my hair, I had little picture of it, but even on the best of days, it would scare a wild goose.

"Thank you, Caleb, my friend."

No sooner had I taken but a few bites of the cake and sipped but once from the wooden cup than I felt sleepy again. Caleb caught me before I fell off my stool. With a friend's gentle hands, he lowered me to a soft wolfskin rug on the cabin floor.

News from Afar

"Why if it ain't ole Johnny! Good to see you up and around, friend."

I smiled at the clerk in the Mansfield Mercantile. It felt good to be on my feet again, even if the earth beneath me still felt a bit wobbly.

"Yup," the clerk continued, "Caleb was in and said you were one sick old rascal. Picked up by some Indians, he said. Glad you still got your scalp on your head."

"I offered it to them," I answered, "but they said they saw better straw and wild weeds in any old turkey's nest."

The clerk laughed loudly. It sounded like music to my ears. Laughter is a special gift sent from the Lord.

"Say, Johnny, did you know you are written about in the newspapers all the way across the world?"

"Now I'm sure you can tell a better story than that," I said.

"I'll swallow a chicken whole if I'm not telling you the truth. Some fella stopped by here a few weeks ago and left a clipping. Said it came all the way from England. It was published in a report.''

Perhaps the clerk was not trying to joke me. ''You say the fellow left the clipping here?''

''He sure enough did. Told me to give it to you the next time you stopped by. Just cool your heels for a moment while I find it.''

The clerk began rummaging around the shelves behind the counter. The talk had sparked my curiosity a mite and I was eager to find out what was being said about me across the ocean.

''Here! Here it is, Johnny!''

I read the clipping carefully. Someone living in Philadelphia had written to someone in Manchester, England. The clipping appeared in a report that was published there in Manchester.

''Well, I'll be hornswoggled,'' I mumbled. ''It *is* about me.''

The clipping read:

> There is in the western country a very extra-ordinary missionary . . . A man has appeared to be almost independent of corporal wants and sufferings. He goes barefooted, can sleep anywhere, in house or out of house, and live upon the coarsest and most scanty fare. He has actually thawed the ice with his bare feet.
>
> He procures what books he can, [then] travels into the remote settlements, and lends them wherever he can find readers, and sometimes divides a book into two or three parts for more extensive distribution and usefulness.
>
> This man for years past has been in the employ-ment of bringing into cultivation, in numberless places in the wilderness, small patches (two or three acres) of ground, and then sowing apple seeds and rearing nurseries.
>
> These become valuable as the settlements approximate.

It went on to say that the profits of the whole were intended for the purpose of enabling me to print spiritual writings and distribute them through the western settlements of the United States.

I looked up and shook my head in disbelief. The clerk was still smiling.

"Yup, sure nice to have somebody famous around here," he said. "Just think of it. Folks all the way across the sea know about our own Johnny. You're quite a fellow, all right, quite a fellow."

"Go on with you, friend. Save your teasing for someone else. Now if you want to read something worthwhile, I'll leave a few clippings here myself.

"Yes, Johnny Appleseed, ever planting seeds of faith just as you plant your seeds for apples. You are truly quite a fellow."

"Quite a fellow." the clerk's tone of voice was admiring and kind. But I know not everyone held me in the same regard. Even my half sister Persis, who had come to live in Perryville with her husband and children, often scolded me. It was gentle scolding, but scolding just the same.

"Look at you, my fine brother!" Persis declared often. "Your bones hang together like an old skeleton. Your cheeks are hollow, your eyes are beady, and you dress as if you're wearing everyone's castaways. Do I not feed you a full meal each time you eat with us? I order you a new wool shirt and you give it away. When someone gives you boots in exchange for your seeds, you find someone else who needs boots, and you give yours away. You are completely, utterly hopeless, Johnny."

I gave my sister a warm hug. "And you put up with me just the same, don't you?"

Persis laughed. "I have to. The children are forever asking when you'll be coming to stay with us. Those girls love the ribbons you bring. For weeks after you leave, they are still tying their hair in new ways. You spoil them all.''

''That's why it's a good thing I never had kids of my own, I reckon.''

''You belong to everybody, John Chapman. When you stay any place, you're a part of the family.''

Persis' words gave me a good feeling inside. There were times when I wondered if maybe I should have found me a girl and settled down. But such thoughts flew away quickly. I liked being able to pick up and go whenever I took the notion. When I longed for a home-cooked meal and family chatter, I could visit any cabin I wished. Folks were always grateful for news of the territory. After a tasty meal, we all sat around a blazing fire and talked long into the night. Yes, in a sense, I was a part of many families.

One morning after bidding farewell to my sister and her lively brood, I started hiking along Mohicanville Road. It was a cheerful morning with breezes dancing through woodland trees and the birds singing their best songs. Suddenly I noticed something moving off the side of the road a bit. I slowed my step. People might be telling stories about Johnny Chapman wrestling with bears, but that's all those tales were—big stories. I had no wish to meet up with any unfriendly varmit looking for a juicy lunch.

It was not a bear that had caught my eye in the woods. It was a horse! Such a woebegone creature I had never seen before in my life. If only Persis might have seen this sight! My dear sister would have started counting every bone—and she could have done just that because every single one of them showed. As I walked around the animal, the horse ignored me. In truth, the poor thing had no strength.

''You are a sight for sore eyes,'' I declared, patting

the thin, sparse mare. "If another breeze comes along, it just might take you along with it."

As I stroked the horse's neck and back, she let out a weak whinny. She turned slightly, seeking out my hand with her nose.

"Hungry, are you? Well, I'm not surprised. I wonder when you last had a full meal. Bet you were just left out here to die by yourself, weren't you?"

A dry tongue licked my hand. The eyes of the poor creature looked dazed and tired. I took a few steps forward, then turned back.

"Come on with you, friend. You may be as skinny as the blade on a pitchfork, but I can't be carrying you on my back. There's a clear water stream not far from here. I fancy there are some farmers in the neighborhood who might be willing to share a few bits of hay."

Slowly the horse lumbered forward. Her head drooped as she walked. It might have been from physical weakness. Yet I sensed that at one time this animal was proud and powerful. Years of work had beaten her down. Unable to be of further use to her master, the horse was turned loose. Now she was alone, frightened, trying to stay alive.

"Hurry along with you," I ordered. "We'll just be seeing what can be done to regain your strength. I suppose I'll have to be giving you a name. Had a mule named Sally once. A better pal a man could not hope for. Stayed by me until her last days. But I think I'll call you something different. Gillyflower. That's it. My favorite kind of apple. Gillyflower. Well, come on, Gillyflower. Time's not for wastin'."

Travels with Gillyflower

My, that old gray mare could eat! In the weeks and months after I found her, Gillyflower filled out so you couldn't see a bone if you squinted. And it didn't surprise me at all when I discovered what her favorite food was. Oats? No. Hay? Not hardly. Sugar blocks? Nope, although she sure didn't turn none of those away.

Apples! Yes, Gillyflower took to apples like she knew they were her name. Morning, afternoon, nighttime—Gillyflower was always ready to munch on an apple.

"The sweetest and best of all God's fruits, aren't they, partner?" I'd ask. Not much for answering, Gillyflower would simply poke her long nose around my pockets, looking for another juicy snack.

On the road, Gillyflower was a loyal companion. Never did I ride her. She was my partner. Around her middle I tied bushel bags of seeds. I made special loops for my kettle, cooking pan, and hoe. Sometimes they all clattered together as we walked. I stepped to the musical beat, making up songs as I went.

> Oh, my name is Johnny Chapman,
>   Some call me Appleseed,
> My friend beside me is Gillyflower,
>   Never known for speed . . .
> We travel 'cross the countryside
>   Sowing seeds in sod,
> If you haven't time to say hello
>   Give us just a nod!

Clink, clatter, clatter, clink—the kettle bounced against the cooking pan. I stroked Gillyflower's neck as she trudged slowly beside me. Again I felt the urge to sing.

> We know each dusty path and road,
>   We know each hillside spring,
> We hear the songs of birds above,
>   We cannot help but sing . . .
> We sing in praise to God, our King,
>   Who rules with love and power,
> We hope someday that we might say
>   I'm Chapman, and this is Gillyflower!

Nonsense rhymes flowed freely from my lips, yet the songs hurried the days by quickly. Now and then Gillyflower whinnied in a rather painful way. But I simply made up one more verse to the melody I chanted.

It was dusk when I strolled along the familiar path into Green Township. My apple tree orchards were full there, and I hastened my step. In other places where I held nurseries, the trees were not always plentiful. But those in Green Township were always a delight.

 As I stopped to sit a spell on a log beside the road,
I spotted a boy approaching. I recognized him as the
oldest Hunter boy. His pa had died two years before,
and I was eager to know how the family was doing.
If memory served me right, there were eight or nine
children in the family. Not an easy task for a widow
to handle. This oldest one, David, could only be seventeen at the most.

 "Say, there's a good familiar face I'm always glad
to see," I shouted. "Come join an old man for a few
moments' chatter, boy."

 A smile crossed David's face as he neared. I hadn't
realized that the sun was in his eyes and he couldn't
see old Gillyflower and me.

 "Hello, Johnny. Good to see you in these parts."

 For a moment I felt as if I was looking into a mir-
ror. David Hunter's hair was long, black, and parted
in the middle, just like my own. His pants and shirt

were two sizes too big for him, and his bare feet matched my own for dirtiness. But he looked a good ten years older than seventeen.

"Where you coming from, David?"

"Had to go to Mansfield to pay the taxes on our land," he answered.

"How's your ma and the rest of your tribe?"

David stared at his naked toes as he rubbed them into the dry grass around the log. "Ma died two months ago," the boy answered, his tone lowered. "I'm lookin' after us all."

I gulped, not knowing what to say. Since words would not come, I leaned closer to the lad and rested my hand on his shoulder. He looked over at me and tried to force a weak smile.

"We're doin' okay," he said. "We'll make it."

How my heart ached for this young boy. No more than seventeen and a house full of kids to look after.

"David, I knew both your folks. They were God-fearin' people," I offered. "So they're with the angels and the Lord right this moment as we sit talking about them."

"I hope so. I really do hope so."

Gillyflower gave a shake, clattering the kettle and cooking pan again. I rose to soothe her. David walked to the opposite side of the animal and stroked her neck.

"My partner here must like you," I said. "She don't take to just anybody, but I can tell she likes you."

David smiled. He slid a cloth sack off his shoulder. "I've got a few corncakes left if you and your horse want to share them with me. Are you willing?"

I nodded. My stomach had not yet started to rumble for food, but I sensed David Hunter needed to talk. There were problems in his eyes and voice. After an hour, he opened up.

"It's my brothers Aaron and Jake. They're too young to understand what's happened. They think I just want to boss them around. 'You can't tell us what to do!' they always say. 'You're not Pa. You're not Ma!' They just won't listen to me.''

How I longed for just the right words to comfort David, to give him support and direction. But the words would not come. My mouth opened and nothing came out. What courage this boy showed! Surely the Lord had given him extra strength.

"How's your farm doing?" I asked, remembering the Hunters owned a few-acre plot.

Again David shook his head. "Not very good. I don't seem to have Pa's knack for growin' things. Aaron and Jake won't work for me like they worked for Pa.''

Suddenly an idea came upon me. This time the words came easily.

"David, you could grow apple trees on your land. It's good soil and catches the sun. There's plenty of need for apples in this territory. Why, every nursery I've started is turning over a good return.''

"But—but we don't have any money for apple trees, Johnny.''

"That's of no mind. I've a brother-in-law, William Broom, who's tending the nursery nearby. We'll start with about fifty or sixty trees. That will give us a good start.''

David looked dazed and confused. I couldn't blame him. One moment he's chewing on a corncake and the next moment he's planning out an orchard. It was sure enough a bucketful of thinking to throw at a boy. But it seemed the only sound notion.

"I just don't know. We can't pay you for the apple trees—''

"Don't recall that I asked for any pay!" I snapped.

"I wouldn't mind havin' a juicy apple from the first big harvest though. My mouth's waterin' just from the thought of it."

"But Pa never took no charity, Johnny. You're givin' and we're a-takin'. It don't seem right."

"Listen, David, my young man. Your folks were always good to me. I shared meals with them and good conversation as well. A man like me asks no more than that from folks. Now they're gone, leaving me with a debt to their hospitality. I'm tryin' to clear my conscience of the debt I owe. Now if you won't allow me that privilege—"

"Oh, don't get me wrong, Johnny. I sure do appreciate your offer. Lord knows I could use any help I can get."

"Well, the good Lord knows I have a debt to pay, too," I answered. "And I'd sleep a lot easier knowing I was doing something about that debt. Now, do we have a deal?"

David smiled. "Sure enough, Johnny."

We shook hands.

"Now, let's be going to your farm. I want to have a little talk with Aaron and Jake."

David seemed a bit more at ease as we headed to the Hunter homestead. He shared openly, wanting to talk a lot about his pa and ma. The boy had clearly cooped up a lot of thoughts in his mind. He was happy to find a pair of ears who would listen to him. As I listened, I pledged that I would become more of a listener to all folks. Everyone, including me— especially me—always wants to talk. I thought about all the families I'd visited. Sure, they were eager to hear the news, to know who I'd seen and when. But I wondered how many of those folks were looking for someone who would listen to them. People stuck in a cabin day after day, week after week, would probably appreciate having someone stop by to listen a bit. Yes, as I listened to David Hunter, I knew I'd been selfish with my listening in the past. The future was different. *I* would be different.

By the time we neared the Hunter farm, dusk was just settling in. A purple-orange hue coated the canvas of the sky. But the air felt heavy, as if there might be a storm gathering not far away. David opened an old wooden gate off the side of the road. He was just tying it closed when a girl's voice drifted across the countryside.

"David! Da-vid!"

In the distance a form raced toward us. Gillyflower shook, the cooking pan and kettle rattling. David turned to me, fear showing on his face.

"It's my sister, Caroline," he said. "Something must be wrong."

The boy darted forward, pulling the girl into his arms. Tears filled her eyes.

"It's Aaron and Jacob," the girl blurted out. "They ran off last night. We've been looking for them all day. Oh, David, I'm so frightened."

The boy held his sister close, softly stroking her long brown hair. She relaxed a bit, her body not trembling. But as David lifted his head to me, I saw nothing but fear on his face.

Runaways

Over a steaming cup of broth and a platter of mutton stew, I was welcomed to the Hunter table. I could easily see that the work completed by Mr. and Mrs. Hunter before their passing was considerable indeed. The children were orderly and well-behaved. Even the baby, not more than fourteen months old, slept peacefully except for an occasional "coo" or "ga-ga" sound.

"The boys were both there when I checked on everyone in the loft," Caroline explained. "Then tell them what you heard, Peter."

Peter could not have been more than eight years old. But he lifted himself tall on the wooden bench on which he sat.

"I heard somebody moving around," the boy declared. "I asked who it was. 'Go back to sleep!' Aaron told me. And so I did. But even with my eyes closed, I could hear him movin' around. Jake too. I heard them climb down the ladder. The next thing I heard was the front door closing."

Caroline shook her head. "Oh, I wish I'd have heard that," she whispered. "If only I hadn't been so tired last night."

I sipped my broth slowly, amazed at how old beyond her years the girl was. David told me she was only eleven, and here she was caring for a whole family.

"I'm going to go look for them," David announced, rising. "They couldn't get too far."

His words were accompanied by a light pattering sound on the roof. The noise was like a handful of pebbles cascading down the wooden beams. Rain. A light roll of thunder shook the cabin.

"Oh, David, I hate it when you're gone," Caroline moaned.

"We all do," Peter echoed. And the other youthful heads around the table nodded agreement.

"No, your place is here with your family," I announced, setting the empty wooden cup on the table. "Gillyflower and I will go find those runaways."

"We can't ask you to do that," David declared.

"You didn't," I answered. "I just offered."

Caroline rose and crossed to the door. She opened it, letting in a puff of wind that shivered the candlelights on the kitchen table.

"But there's a storm coming," Caroline noted. "Oh, David, what about Aaron and Jacob in this storm? Do you think—"

I crossed to the doorway. "I think it's time I got underway. I'm just obliged for that de-licious hot mutton stew you gave me, Miss Caroline. A man could travel a hundred miles with that kind of meal sloshing around inside of him."

David stepped in front of me. "Johnny, you don't have to do this. Those boys will come home. If they don't, well, it would just serve them right."

"David!" Caroline burst out.

"Now, hold on a moment," I said. "I'm starting to hear angry words. I never did like angry words. Too much love in this house for angry words to be shared." I moved to the doorway, sidestepping David. "Now the good Lord has been kind enough to send me some lightning to light up the nighttime. Why, I could see those two scallywags if they were a mile away. What I'm wanting to know is if there's any special place they might be going."

Caroline looked puzzled. "No, I don't think so."

"Meader's Cave," David said. "That's their own favorite place. They've camped out there sometimes."

"So that's where they go," Caroline said.

"It's just their place," David emphasized. "They never wanted any of you girls trailing them there."

"Who cares where they'd go. Not me."

Ignoring his sister's remarks, David turned to me. "Johnny, I'm not sure you should go there with this rain coming down. That land around there is pretty rough. Those big rocks can slide right out from under you. Anyway, they may not be there at all. If they're as upset as Caroline says, they might really have taken off for good."

"It's a place to start," I offered. "Better than no direction at all. Don't worry about my footing. These old feet of mine haven't given out from under me yet. You just rest easy, and be saying a few prayers if you will."

"We will," Caroline murmured. "We all will."

Once outside, I headed to the barn to find Gillyflower. She'd be surprised we would be setting out at night. Most of the time we traveled in the daytime. When we got ourselves into the open barn-yard, the mule inside Gillyflower came alive. She probably thought I'd taken all my senses and thrown

them into the wind. Streaks of lightning slashed across
the sky, while claps of thunder pounded and rolled
against the land.

"Come on, old partner," I coaxed. "We got some
mighty big work to do before we get any sleep. Come
on." Reluctantly the horse stumbled forward. *Caboom*! Another burst of thunder shook the earth
beneath our feet.

"I'm grateful to you for the lightning, Lord," I
said. "It helps us see the way. But we sure could do
without all this noise as we go."

Although I had never set foot in Meader's Cave,
I knew where it was. It bordered a small lake not far
from one of the northern strips of the Ohio River. In
truth, there weren't too many spots in this territory
I had not traveled more times than I have fingers and
toes. Supposedly an old pioneer named Ambrose
Meader had taken the trek west from New York in
hopes of making his fortune. He ended up with no
more than a hole on a hillside. Folks found his bones
long after the old fellow went to meet his Maker.

"Poor man never did find much out here," someone said. "The least we can do is call his home
Meader's Cave."

That's how the place got its name.

The rain still poured by the time I reached the edge
of the pond which lay about two miles from the Hunter
farm. I could see the cave in the distance. Lightning
lit up the sky, making the cave on the hillside look
like a giant's open mouth. Gillyflower shook. Clatter, bang, clatter, clink.

"No time for songs," I told Gillyflower. "Let's just
hope—"

The words stuck in my throat as I gazed up at the
opening of Meader's Cave. There was a light, a small
flickering light coming from the darkness. I hurried

my steps, carefully planting each step soundly before I took another. Slate rocks dotted the area around the pond shoreline. I had no desire to join any fish.

Boom! Caboom! Thunder roared in my ears. Again and again I wiped the rain from my eyes. At the base of the hillside, I tied Gillyflower to a large dead log.

"Now don't you go wandering away," I admonished the animal. "If I am right, there will be two young boys wanting to find a warm bed tonight."

Securing a firm step, I began climbing the hillside. Mud and sand squished between my toes. Some of the rocks felt sharp and jagged, but my old tired feet were crusted thick from going without boots or shoes.

As the hillside steepened, I leaned forward, grabbing the edge of large rocks for gripping. Yes, I could see the flickering light more clearly now. One candle. That's what it had to be. Just one candle.

My desire to reach the cave rapidly made me careless. Just as I reached a small landing, I thrust myself forward and up. Suddenly I felt myself slipping down the hillside, mud and pebbles coating my whole body. I spit a mouthful of wet dirt from my mouth.

"Slowly," I whispered to myself, remembering the words of Matthew in the Bible. "The spirit indeed is willing, but the flesh is weak."

This time I proceeded with more caution. One mistake is enough for anyone but a fool. A flash of lightning showed me that Gillyflower stood safely at the hillside base. Slowly I began my climb once more.

The minutes seemed like hours as I made my way up the hill. Finally, I reached the cave itself. Winded from the climb, I lay flat against the ground. I slept for a few minutes, but a roll of thunder jerked my head into consciousness. Lifting myself to my feet, I trudged to the cave entrance.

"Aaron," I called. "Jacob. Are you here? Aaron Hunter. Jacob Hunter. Make yourself known."

There was no sight of the candlelight. Had the storm killed the flame? Maybe the two young runaways had gone deeper into the cave.

"Aaron Hunter? Jacob Hunter? It is John Chapman come to find you. Make yourself known to me."

I strained to hear. Raindrops pelted the giant rocks and I could hear the tiny streams rolling down the hillside into the pond below. But there was no other sound. Had there been a light at all? Perhaps my own eyes had played tricks on me. Perhaps I had wanted so badly to see a light that I imagined one.

"Mr. Chap-man? Is that you, Mr. Chapman?"

A young boy's voice broke the human silence within the cave. I squinted, wishing for a streak of lightning to give me vision.

"Yes, it is John Chapman, a friend to your pa and ma and all those who carry the Hunter name. Would that be the both of you?"

"Yes, it is Aaron Hunter and my brother Jake. We had a candle, but it has gone out."

"I cannot see either of you lads in this darkness. Can you see me?"

"We see you when there is lightning. If you step forward, you will be on safe ground. You will be out of the rain."

I was grateful for such an opportunity. Eagerly I entered the cave. A small hand sliding into mine felt good indeed.

"We have a blanket," Aaron whispered. "Some of it is wet, but if you kneel, you will be on it."

I lowered myself, feeling the sudden warmth of two small bodies snuggling to each side. The forms shivered.

"There are many nights when I might enjoy sleeping in such a cave as this," said I. "But this night is not one of them. Surely you might provide a better bed for a weary visitor."

"We didn't know it was going to storm like this," Aaron answered. "Tomorrow we are going to Mansfield."

"But your brother David is already home," I replied.

For the first time the younger Hunter spoke. "We're not going to find David. We're going away from him."

For a moment I did not speak. Then I leaned back against the cave wall, pulling the boys with me.

"Hm-m-m. That's strange. You sound so eager to get away from him, yet he seemed troubled when Caroline told him you had gone."

"He wasn't troubled," Aaron snapped. "He was

happy. He'll be glad to have us gone. Except he'll have two less people to give orders to.''

Again I paused to collect my thoughts. Each time the lightning lit up the world outside the cave opening, the boys shoved themselves closer. When the thunder rolled, I felt as if Jacob and Aaron were climbing inside me.

''That's a funny notion you have about your brother,'' I offered. ''You thinking he'd be glad to have you gone. Why, he was coming here himself before I stopped him. Didn't seem even a mite happy about you being gone. Just looked worried to me. Awful worried.''

This time it was the boys who were quiet for a while. Finally, Aaron stirred against me and I could tell he was looking up at my face—even if he could not see it in the darkness.

''Mr. Chapman, you know about our pa and ma?''

''Um-huh. I was mighty sorry to hear. Your folks were good people, mighty good people.''

''Well, Mr. Chapman, we know you is a religious man. Pa and Ma both told us.''

''You tell stories,'' Jacob injected. ''Stories about God and angels.''

''I admit to that,'' I answered.

Aaron continued. ''Well, when Pa died we all hurt bad inside. When Ma took sick, we all prayed for her to get well. You always told us that God is listening and answers all our prayers.''

''That's true,'' I said. ''I believe that He does and I share the Word with others.''

Suddenly Aaron pulled away. ''Well, we prayed to God that our ma would get better, and then she died. God didn't answer our prayers. He didn't listen.''

Gently I pulled the sad boy back to my side. ''Oh,

13

On to In

Peace returned to the Hunt
was in the territory I stopped
a few years, David displayed
three hundred trees.

"I couldn't have done it w
he said. "All these trees come fr
me with."

"It is the Lord who gran
answered. "Without the se
nothing. We are but His serv

But with the passing of year
an itching to travel once more.
ing from their travels west sp

"Still mostly wilderness," on
to watch out for wolves and
night. But there's an adventu
a bit too civilized for my likii

The old man spoke my lang
sit forever on the old stump. N
parcel of meat and bone likes to

yes, lad. God listened. But sometimes, just sometimes,
God has to say no."

Thunder rumbled outside. Slowly I rubbed the
backs of both boys who sat beside me. Their shiver-
ing had stopped. Sleep was beginning to set in.

"Whoa, now, gentlemen. This cave floor may seem
soft enough for a bed to your bones. But as for me,
I want something else. Give me a good carved-out
tree stump or a mossy grass patch. But no caves for
me. Now I've got a fine friendly horse waiting at the
bottom of this hill. Usually no one rides her back cause
I use her for carrying my seeds and tools. But tonight
is special. I think old Gillyflower would be a mite
pleased to have two young boys on her back."

"Go back home?" Aaron said defiantly. "Not us."

"Um-m-m," I murmured, rising to my feet.
"Well, I'm afraid that's where I'm going. That mutton stew Miss Caroline made tonight coated my ribs
just fine. I noticed she made a whole kettleful and I'm
thinkin' another plateful would taste awful good."

"Caroline made mutton stew?" Jacob asked.

"She sure did," I answered. "And that hot turkey
broth was mighty tasty, too."

"Oh, let's go home," Jacob begged. "It's so cold
out here—and dark. I'm scared, Aaron. I told you
I wasn't, but I am."

"I knew it," the older boy exclaimed. "I knew I
shouldn't have brought you along. You're just little.
You want to go back and let David order you
around?"

"I wonder why David does that," I asked aloud.
"Why should he give all the orders?"

"He's just trying to keep us together," Jacob burst
out. "He's the oldest."

"Um-m-m. Now that sounds sensible enough," I

said. "With your pa a
to give the orders."

"But it's not fair, M
was losing force. "It's
time."

"That's probably tru
I've found? It's not alw
I bet there isn't anyon
pa and ma back to give
has to do what he has
he has to give the ord

For a long time no o
to his feet. "Come on,
you still take us, Mr.

"The offer is still the
partner Gillyflower is,

Grabbing the boys'
the cave entrance. For
the night.

"The rain's let up a b
of yours feel good whe

"I just want some c
answered.

happening. Anyway, surely this Indiana land needed apple trees too.

"I'm leaving old Gillyflower with you," I told David Hunter. "I'll be a-following the river into Indiana. No place for a horse in an old dugout. I'll be obliged if you take good care of this animal. She and I've been partners quite a spell now."

"I will, Johnny," David promised. "And you take good care of yourself."

I wasn't about to paddle into Indiana empty-handed. So I filled my boat with wet mud and tree-moss covering a full load of appleseed.

If ever there was a river with twists and turns, it's the Maumee, bred of a union between the St. Mary's and the St. Joseph. I knew where I was headed. Fort Wayne. Travelers back to Ohio called the town "a frontier wildpost of French and Indian settlers." Not much of a business spot for a place boasting 150 residents in 1830, but it had potential. Potential. I always liked that word. The promise of something good to come. A better future.

Fort Wayne, named after the old Revolutionary War general of whom my pa spoke so long ago. When I tied up my dugout to a landing place below the old fort, I felt at home. A cool breeze off the river seemed to whisper, "John Chapman. Welcome." Yes, there was a good feeling about being here in Fort Wayne.

I stretched my arms into the sunlight. Skinny, most would call them. But I wondered how many men of fifty-six years could paddle a craft half as fast as I had been. The muscles were still strong and firm. The Lord had blessed me greatly.

It soon became clear to me that Fort Wayne was a mixture of many things. To the Indians, the town was known as Kekionga or "Meeting of the Ways." It was Miami town to the French-Canadians and half-breeds. But for us Americans, it was Fort Wayne because our own Mad Anthony Wayne won the land for America.

I had no wish to live inside the town itself, so I headed quickly for the outlying regions. Land in Jay County was selling for two dollars an acre, a bargain indeed. The soil was ripe for apple trees and I didn't waste a day in getting seeds planted.

Days slipped quickly into months, then years. Seeds became saplings, then sturdy sentinels of the earth. Soon juicy fruit loaded each branch.

I was not the only soul around Fort Wayne who felt a love for the apple tree. This noble prince of the Miami Indian nation, Chief Richardville, came often from his reservation to visit the site of his birth in Fort Wayne. The site was marked by a single old apple tree, and the chief held it in special regard. Each of his visits brought out all the area citizens, eager to admire the Indian in all his rich jewels, headdress, and robes.

My good friend William Worth told me of a morning when the chief was coming for a visit. Strangely enough, whenever I visited Will, I stayed in an old deserted Indian hut on his land. It was not his wish however.

"Stay in the house with us, Johnny," Will said often. "Why, there's no bed in the hut, not a decent chair or bed. I don't want you sleeping on the floor."

"Don't fuss with me, friend. Many a night I've slept under the open sky, gazing up at the stars. A bed just makes a man spoiled and soft. I'll be fine."

When we went to see Chief Richardville, I knew I had to say a few words to the man myself. Will was a bit nervous about such a thought.

"I'm not certain what the chief will do," my friend

said. "Maybe if you'd like to wear a pair of my pants and a fresh shirt—"

I held up my hand for silence. "It is not clothes that make us what we are. It is the soul and spirit within us. I will be certain to scrub myself clean however, so as not to cause you embarrassment."

Will simply laughed.

I stood with a small cluster of people waiting for the chief's arrival. He came riding in, mounted on a noble white mare of sharp eye and strong frame. His braves surrounded him until he dismounted and walked toward the tree.

I watched Chief Richardville as he stood silently before the worn, weary apple tree. Truly the warmth and sensitivity in the air could be felt by everyone nearby. This noble, rich, and powerful leader paying respect to the place of his birth. As he turned to leave, I stepped forward.

"My name is John Chapman," I said. "I just wanted—"

The chief motioned for me to stop speaking and I did. "You are the sower of seeds," he said. "The man who plants apple trees."

Surely the surprise showed on my face. "Yes, that is what I do. But I must confess, I had no part in planting your tree."

The chief nodded and smiled. "No, but I believe it is one of the few in this territory you did not plant. I am happy to know you, John of the appleseeds. Please keep doing your work. You make our land more beautiful and help to feed our people. What you do is good."

I nodded and backed away. There was goodness in the face of Chief Richardville and kindness in his heart. It did not surprise me at all that an apple tree marked the site of his birth.

I was grateful that Persis, my half sister, saw reason to move her family west to Indiana. Her husband was eager to work, and I was happy to have the help with my planting.

Much as I coaxed, I could not persuade my half sister Sally to join us in Indiana. She and her husband, John Whitney, called the lower Muskingum Valley in Ohio "their own paradise." When I returned to Ohio, I always stayed with them for a week or two.

On one such visit, lightning struck a huge black oak tree and split it from its top to its very roots. Many of the fragments were converted to comfortable sized rails which we neatly stacked not far from the house.

"Don't quite understand why the Lord should punish me this way," my brother-in-law complained. "Sally and I live by the Good Book, and we bring our kids up in the same way. Don't quite understand the Lord when He throws us such a trouble as this. And with all you've done for growing trees, you'd think He might spare those we have around us."

"No, John, I think you have a misguided way of looking at this whole situation," I said, measuring a short length of the timber. "You and your sons have worked mighty hard to clear this land and build a fine farm. Isn't that true, my friend?"

John nodded. "We're happy here, if that's what you're saying."

"Making wood rails is mighty hard work. That's true too, isn't it?"

"Yup."

"Well, as I see it, the good Lord has blessed you with a fine bunch of sons. He led you to the place and helped you build a fine big farm. But with all this work your boys put in to build this farm, the Lord decided to help you out. He sent His lightning to split that old tree and give you a fine set of wood rails. Now that's the way I see it.''

John Whitney rubbed his chin as he stared at the stacked timber. ''Well, I've always been grateful to God for lookin' over me and my family. I know He's given us many blessings. But I sure never did hear of Him making rails for anybody before.''

I smiled. ''The Lord works in mysterious ways,'' I answered. ''I guess this is one of them.''

Life in Fort Wayne

"Nothin' grows faster than a family of rabbits in the woods."

I remember my pa saying that so many years ago in Massachusetts. Well, Pa never did see Fort Wayne or I'm thinking he would have had to change his tune a note or two. Every time I headed into town for supplies, there was another new store built and a few more cabins.

"You ought to be livin' a mite closer to town," folks would tell me. "You don't get to be a part of things goin' on."

Well, there was some truth to that and a lot of falsehood.

The truth was that there were surely a lot of fine folks I was meeting who came to settle. God-fearin' and God-lovin' folk who read the Bible and followed its ways.

But there were a speck too many of the other kind as well. Their favorite time was when the Indians came to town on trading days. Sometimes the friendly

Indian men came to pick up their government annuities, and there was always a band of scalawags wanting to share in money that didn't belong to them.

One night I stayed in town. It was a foul evening with the wind shaking the trees until the leaves begged for mercy.

"You hold over until tomorrow," Tillie Clark warned me. "We'll not be sending you out to face any Indiana storm. Why, as skinny as you are, you'd be blown over the moon!"

"I'm not feared of any storm," I answered. "Every now and then the good Lord has to shake us up a bit here on earth. Otherwise, we might get to thinking we're a mite more important than we are."

"That's all well and good, Johnny," Roger Clark said, scratching a full face of whiskers. "But I'm also thinking the good Lord might just send a storm to test our good sense. It seems to me that anybody who'd be heading into the woods on a night like this just might make the Lord wonder about that man's good sense."

"Anyway, I'll be putting these apples you brought me to good use," Mrs. Clark declared. "If you'll be staying with us tonight, I'll have time to make a couple tasty apple pies for eating tomorrow."

I smiled. "Well, I sure don't want the good Lord thinking I don't have any sense," I offered, "and I sure do hate the thought of missing any of your pie, dear woman, so I believe I'll be staying the night."

The Clarks were a good family, with two children, Abraham and Alice. We feasted on a delicious turkey, and Mrs. Clark made certain I had an extra helping of corn bread spread heavily with apple butter.

Around a warm fire in the evening, I shared readings from the Bible.

"Tell us the story about the Good Samaritan," Abraham requested.

"Oh, you always want to hear that story," Alice protested. "I like the one where Jesus made the dead man alive again. That's the best story of all."

I nodded, opening the pages in the light of the crackling fire. "Such an argument is easily solved. What if we hear both stories?"

"That's fine with me," answered Abraham.

"I like both of them," Alice agreed.

We had finished the Good Samaritan and had reached the point where Lazarus had been raised, when we heard loud shouting outside. Roger Clark leaped to the front door and threw it open.

"What is it?" he asked a man running by.

"The militia! Those traders have come in and got the Indians angry and drunk. The militia have been called in."

Roger Clark turned to me. "Will you stay here with the wife and children, Johnny? I know how you feel about such things, but I've got to see if there is any danger. I would appreciate your watching over things here."

"They'll be safe here," I told Roger Clark. "You do what you have to do. I'll not be leaving your family until you return."

"I'm much obliged to you."

As we closed the door and returned to the hearth, Abraham looked up at me. "Why wouldn't you want to go with Pa, Johnny?"

I gazed into the fire, then laid a hand on Abraham's shoulder. "A man must listen to God's voice, as He directs our way. He speaks to us through the Good Book here, and then we know what to do."

"But Pa went," Alice said. "Is he bad?"

I shook my head. "God speaks to your pa, too. He may not tell your pa the same thing He tells me."

Abraham looked defiant. "Yes, but why does God

tell those traders to cheat and hurt the Indians?''

I picked up the Bible and sat down in the old rocker. ''Oh, that isn't God speaking to those people. That is the Devil, and he has a loud and ugly voice. If those traders don't listen to God, then they will listen to the Devil.''

''I don't think the Devil ever talks to me,'' Alice announced proudly.

''Um-m-m,'' I said, rubbing my chin. ''Has your ma ever asked you to do something and you did something else?''

''I don't —''

''Remember last week, sister? Ma told you to pick berries and you went swimming instead? You listened to the Devil!''

Alice glanced at her mother, who sat quietly darning in a nearby rocker. The woman did not speak, but her eyes looked soft and sad.

Then suddenly Alice raised her finger at her brother. ''Yes, and what of you and the Rudisill boys? Pa asked you to chop wood and you all went over to see the new mares in the north pasture.''

This time it was Abraham's turn to feel foolish. His face reddened in the glow of the fire.

''Let us be honest,'' I said. ''There are times when we all know God is speaking to us, but we listen to another voice. It is not as it should be, but He understands us better than anyone. He only hopes that it will not happen often.''

Mrs. Clark looked over at me. Her busy fingers stopped moving. ''I am grateful that you come here to remind us,'' she said softly. ''Folks say that having good John Chapman stop by for a visit is just like having the preacher over for Sunday dinner. He always eats with a hearty appetite and shares cheerful news of the Lord.''

"They are both enjoyable tasks in this house, ma'm, and I'm happy to hear you share such kind words."

Fort Wayne was a bustling little town as the years rolled by. Settlers passed through on their way west, but many took a liking to the folks of Fort Wayne and decided to stay.

There was a big celebration in '35 when the northern part of the canal through the town was opened. Cannon exploded for days, telling the world about the event. More politicians came to town than there are quills on a porcupine's back.

"Another gateway to the west is open," one stout fellow in a suit which was burstin' shouted at the folks. "We are witnessing a new era, the likes of which our country has never seen. We are history on the move."

History didn't seem to be moving nearly as fast as the fancy young girls who paraded down the Fort Wayne streets. Each one of these thirty-one lovely misses wore a banner naming a state of the union. It was a fine sight to see, all right, and the ladies smiled and waved at everyone. I could not help but think of my pa, fighting for freedom and liberty long before there was anything such as a United States of America. Made me feel a bit proud.

And then the *Indiana*, the first packet vessel to come along the canal, was towed along. The cheers went up loud and long. Rifles were fired, followed by happy shouts of boys and girls.

Thinking about wild and happy shouts made me think of the presidential campaign of 1840.

If I thought I'd seen and heard politicians when the canal opened up, I had no thought how many more would come hollerin' and whoopin' to Fort Wayne when good old William Henry Harrison took to running for the presidency. William Henry hailed from neighboring Ohio, and it was the first time anyone from the West took to shooting for the highest office in the United States.

Bonfire Tonight!
Political Rally in the City Square at 2 P.M.

Banners and posters hung from every post and sidewall. Men paraded carrying blazing torches, gathering around to hear someone talk about the great wonders of the honorable Mr. Harrison.

Everyone wore buckeyes, the nuts that came from chestnut trees. Girls wore buckeye necklaces and bracelets. Men twirled buckeye canes and smoked from buckeye pipes. Yes, Ohio was the "Buckeye State" and had its own candidate for President of the United States. The folks from Indiana shared their pride.

"You should run for president!" someone shouted at me while we stood in front of a blazing bonfire waiting to hear another speaker. "We could all wear apples around our necks, have cider parties, and feast on apple pie, Johnny."

I laughed, amused at the very thought of me running for any office. "I'm afraid most of my supporters would like to see an apple in my mouth," I shouted back. "That way I could not be giving any speeches."

No, there was no voice inside of me saying I should be running for any political office. Oh, I liked people well enough. Nothing pleased me more than sharing my seeds and young trees with folks. But I had no hankerin' for running for public office.

Not unless someone needed a fellow to be president of the Indiana Orchards.

With the good Lord's help, that's a job I might be able to handle.

15

Midnight Visitor

A white, searing flame shot across the sky. Moments later, a clap of thunder loud enough to scare the skin off a wild wolf! Whirling blasts of rain pound against my cabin walls and the wind shakes the whole house.

Summer storm.

Nothing can slip up on you so suddenly as a powerful storm in the Midwest. Bright rays of sun can fill a warm afternoon sky. Without any warning at all, clouds slither into position and turn the entire world into wild confusion.

It was on such a night that I wakened from sleep to hear heavy hammering on my cabin door. At first I thought that rain had turned to sleet. But when the pounding continued, I slid from my bed and crossed the room.

Opening the door a sliver so as to prevent the rain from blowing in, I peered into the darkness outside. Nothing could I see. As I started to close the door, I felt a sudden weight against it. The wind, I thought, and I shoved harder.

Lightning filled the sky, lighting up the entire world in front of my cabin. In that quick moment I glanced down to the ground below. Then I discovered the cause of the weight against the door. It was the body of a man.

Hurriedly I pulled the door completely open, reaching low to lend support to the fellow. A gust of rain blinded me for an instant as I pulled the man's body inside.

"Who are you?" I asked, wondering if the man could hear me at all. "Are you hurt or sick?"

No answer. Slowly I pulled the body across the floor. He was not a small man in any way. For a moment I longed for the days when I could lift a log and roll it easily. The days were gone, long gone. Now I fumbled awkwardly, attempting to make the man comfortable before the fireplace which still claimed a few red-gold embers.

"Uhm-ah-ha . . ."

The sound within my visitor was weak and unclear. But I was grateful to hear it anyway. It was the first real sign that he was even alive. I threw a few more good-sized cedar logs into the fireplace, then hurried to get a few rags to soak the wetness from the stranger's skin.

Crack!

Another boom of thunder rumbled across the sky. At the same time, a fresh curtain of rain coated the entire room. Scrambling to my feet, I stepped to the front door and bolted it.

"Ahgh-agh—"

The sound was louder this time and I thought I saw the body move with its own power. As new flames captured the fresh logs and cast a brightness to the room, I could see my visitor more clearly.

He was a Negro man, maybe of forty years or

thereabouts. His torn shirt revealed strong arms and a wide chest. His shoulders were broad, as well.

"Can you hear me?" I shouted, moving closer and wiping a few final drops from the man's face. "Who are you?"

Slowly, ever so slowly, the heavy eyelids opened. The pools beneath were red and watery. Was the man sick? Perhaps he had been attacked. Stories were common enough of wolves or bears leaping upon unsuspecting travelers along the woodland paths. As the warmth of the blazing fire filled the room, I struggled to free the man from his soaked shirt. As he leaned forward to assist my efforts, he suddenly let out an uncontrollable cry. By the firelight, I gazed down at the strong back and noted the deep, ugly‾ slashes which cut into the flesh.

"Merciful God!" I mumbled, realizing that the wounds had been made by a whip. Quickly I moved to my bed, withdrew the blanket and wrapped it around my friend's shoulders.

"Hm-m-m . . . ," the poor fellow whimpered, the softest and gentlest sound he had made since being brought inside my cabin. His hand fell over my own and squeezed it slightly. Then, his head slipping to one side, the stranger fell quickly asleep.

Spreading the blanket evenly over the man's body, I tossed another log onto the fire. There was little point in trying to hold further conversation with the stranger. He was clearly too tired to talk, or else had no such desire.

In truth, I confess that I slept little for the rest of the night. After many hours, the storm slipped away. Once again the outside world was still.

But inside my small cabin, I could hear the slow, heavy sound of the stranger breathing. Occasionally he would toss and roll a bit, but I remained in my own bed. "Who have You brought to my door?" I whispered into my pillow. "Lord, what stranger in the night have You left with me?"

I met the first rays of morning sunlight with eagerness and joy. Even with the cornmeal mush bubbling in a tin pan over the fire, my midnight guest did not stir from his deep sleep. Only when I jostled him from side to side did he begin to make sounds of life. After a few mumblings and grumblings, he sat up and looked around.

I handed him a tin platter of hot cornmeal mush with wild raspberries heaped along the side. He took the food eagerly, shoveling it into his mouth with the wooden spoon he gripped tightly in his hand.

The lightness of the day gave me a better opportunity to study the stranger sitting on the hearth. He was big boned, but the lack of flesh on his frame made me think he had not eaten full meals for a long time. His muscles were firm and solid, accustomed to heavy work. The blanket I had wrapped around his upper body had slipped off. Daylight gave the wide, deep scars on his back even an uglier look. Some vicious whip had torn away the skin, leaving a quilted crisscross of horrid sores.

"Are you from Indiana?" I asked.

The man lifted his head, staring at me, examining my every move. He shook his head from side to side.

"May I call you by a name?"

It was clear the man heard me. Yet he did not say a word. He simply looked and stared.

"Have you a name?" I asked again, this time the tone in my voice showing annoyance and impatience.

Once more there came no reply.

Despite the man's size, I had no fear of him. But why would he not speak? I stood, almost ready to walk to the front door, unbolt it, and send the stranger out into the morning air. It was then I recalled Hebrews 13:2—"Be not forgetful to entertain strangers: for thereby some have entertained angels unawares."

Instead of my previous thought, I stepped forward, took my guest's plate, and replenished his food. This time he smiled, bowing graciously with his head, and returned to his eating. I filled his tin cup with hot honeymilk.

"You'll want as much of this as you can get," I offered. "The Bible tells us that honey and milk is heavenly food."

This time the man smiled. He lifted his cup as if to toast me, and took a long gulp.

Then I heard the sounds of horses. My stranger heard the sounds at about the same time. Quickly he stood, rushed to me, and took my hand. His eyes looked woeful, solemn and pleading. For the first time I knew the reason that he was silent. He could not speak.

Pulling the blanket around his broad shoulders, the man hobbled frantically around the room. He seemed to be dazed. I hurried to the stranger and grabbed his arm. Within moments, I led him outside, circled my cabin, and threw open the door leading to the underground cellar.

"Stay down there and be quiet," I ordered. "Don't make the slightest sound."

The last thing I saw before closing the cellar door was the man staring helplessly out at me. But there was the trace of a faithful smile on his face. Yes, this man trusted me. I prayed this trust would not be wasted.

As I came around the corner to the front of my cabin, two men on horseback approached. I recognized Franklin Webster, who owned a farm a few miles over. The other fellow, a thin pale man with a mustache greased to his skin, was not familiar.

"Hello, Johnny!"

I nodded. "Howdy, Franklin. What brings you calling so early in the morning?"

"I do," the moustached stranger said, not waiting for Franklin's reply. "This ain't a courtesy call, Mr. Chapman."

The man's manner was proud and powerful. Clearly he was not a man to waste time. I knew Franklin Webster to be a meek sort of fellow, not easily riled. But I did not appreciate him being ignored in such a way.

"It doesn't have to be any courtesy call for a fellow to be courteous," I countered. "Folks in these parts are accustomed to treat each other with a mite of respect. That's true enough, isn't it, Franklin?"

"Sure is, Johnny."

"Well, I ain't got time for you two neighbors to be bending your jaws about how much you Northerners love each other. I've got business here."

"And what business might that be?"

"You ain't seen a good-for-nothin' colored man, have you? He's a hunk of a fellow, uglier than a gutted steer and smellin' worse than a litter of skunks."

I looked up at the man on the horse, his face curled in a hateful sneer as he spoke. Clean he was on the outside, but I sensed the dirty devil that lived within.

And I thought about the poor hungry soul I had hiding back in the cellar. Those eyes, those sad, tired eyes belonged to a man of goodness who had suffered. There was something mighty peculiar about this whole situation.

"I have seen no one by the description you have given me," I answered honestly. "Neither do I know by name who I am talking to. Folks hereabouts are

accustomed to introducing each other. I believe you
called my by my name a mite earlier. I reckon it's
time I heard yours.''

"The name's Rob Collier, come from Georgia looking for three runaway slaves.''

"They belong to you?''

"No, I'm just a-lookin' for the reward that goes
from bringin' these no good coloreds back. Caught
two of the varmints already, but the third broke away
from us. Moses Carter is his name. Don't do much
talkin' since we yanked out his tongue.''

I swallowed deeply, horrified at what I was hearing. "You 'yanked' out his tongue?''

Mr. Collier grinned. "It's got to be done
sometimes. These coloreds get to answering back when
they shouldn't. Usually the whip cures such notions.
But there are those like Moses Carter who will take
whippings to the bone and still not keep quiet.''

Again, my thoughts flew to the man in my fruit
cellar. Oh, how is it that such suffering and pain can
be exchanged among God's creatures?

"What was it Moses Carter said that would be
cause for taking away his means of speaking?'' I asked.

"Mr. Ronson, his master, was planning to sell two
of Moses' boys. Moses didn't want to give them up
because they were but six and eight.''

I glanced at Franklin Webster. His head drooped
in shame and sorrow. It was clear he had no desire
to be with our visitor a minute longer than he had to.

"Well, Mr. Collier, like I said before, no man of
the description you gave has crossed my path. But I'll
be more than a mite honest with you. If he did, I'd
not be letting you or Mr. Ronson know about it. I
see no cause that gives anyone the right to mar a man
in any way.''

Mr. Collier's eyes squinted in anger. He held his reins tightly.

"Moses Carter belongs to Mr. Ronson. You Northerners keep interferin' in the way we live. Got railroads smuggling our slaves up here. We're downright tired of the way you weak-livered varmints snake our slaves away."

"Mr. Collier, I never have rightly understood how one man can own another. The way I read it, the Word of God tells me we are all His creatures, no one any better or worse than the rest, and certainly no one belonging to another. Now I have a heap of chores to do around this place and I'll not be getting them done talking to you."

Franklin Webster shook the reins he held in his hands. His horse whinnied as the man turned in his saddle.

"I've got chores of my own, Mr. Collier," Franklin said. "Sorry we bothered you, Johnny."

Collier looked surprised. "What's wrong with you fools? Help me find this no-good colored trash and I might be able to get you a part of the reward."

"I'm a little choosy about how I earn my money, Mr. Collier," I answered.

Franklin nodded. "A lot of us are. I told you I'd bring you to the next farm and I've done that. Wish I'd have asked you more questions first. Might have saved me some time. I'll be seeing you in town, Johnny."

"Take care of yourself, Franklin."

With a light jerk of his reins, my neighbor bounded off. I turned to go inside, ignoring Mr. Collier.

"Say, Chapman, you sure you don't want to help find this mongrel. This cabin of yours could use some fixin' up. Pretty rundown place. Those trees yonder look mighty healthy though. I hear you got a way with raising trees.''

There is a point where any person grows weary of being friendly to strangers. No longer did I feel like wasting time with the likes of the visitor on horseback who decorated the front of my home.

"Mr. Collier, I believe in being honest. The Good Book tells us to put away lying, speak every man truth with his neighbor. Now, in truth, I don't like what you do and I don't like what Mr. Ronson does either. It would be just as well if you found your way off this little homestead of mine. You don't seem to find it too pleasant a place anyway, so I think I'd be obliged if you took your business elsewhere.''

Mr. Collier shook his head, looking at me as if I was some kind of fool taken leave of his senses. But I stared at him firm and steady. Finally, he pulled his horse away and galloped off. I was glad to see the last of him.

Quickly I turned and raced to the fruit cellar. How my heart cried for the poor man hiding. I could not help but think of the Moses of so long ago and how he suffered, too. Why is it God speaks so clearly to us all and yet we do not hear?

"Moses! Moses Carter! Are you there?''

From the darkness the big man moved forward. His eyes squinted in the sunlight, but his face reflected his fear.

"It's all right, Moses. Mr. Collier is gone. You will stay here with me as long as you wish.''

He followed my lips, almost as if he couldn't hear. Gradually his expression changed from confusion to trust. I led the man back into the cabin.

"You must not go out of the cabin unless I know. There is much work to be done inside to keep you busy. I don't have many visitors to my little place here.

It could certainly use cleaning if you're inclined toward such work.''

Moses nodded.

For the next three days Moses Carter stayed with me. He was welcome company. It gave me a chance to cleanse the ugly wounds on his back and cover them with herb dressings. The man ate heartily, enjoying every bite. A healthy glow came back to his face.

In the evening I read aloud the joyful news of the Good Book. It all seemed so new to him, as if he had never heard the wonderful tidings the Bible brings. It brought back long-ago memories to me of my early days in Massachusetts. I could almost hear old Reverend Williams himself as the wind swept across the plain and shivered my cabin.

''Know the Lord,'' he would command us as we sat listening in the church. ''Know the Lord. Listen to His message and believe on Him. Do not stray from the path He leads you along and He shall be waiting for you at the end of the road.''

How the eyes of Moses Carter would widen when I read the Scriptures. Truly this man who shared my home and my food was a man of goodness. Thus, it pained me even more that his tongue should have been taken, never allowing him to speak again. It was not an easy task holding back the hate I felt for this Mr. Ronson, a man I had never met, and Mr. Collier, whom I barely knew. What kind of men could these be to so injure and defile another? Over and over I reminded myself of God's feelings about hating. Surely if Jesus, our Savior, could forgive those who put Him to death, I could forgive my own enemies. I prayed for the strength to do that.

Just as he had come, Moses Carter departed in the middle of the night. It was a silent exit, perhaps

because the kindly, gentle man did not know how to
bid farewell.

But as I looked at the wooden kitchen table, I saw
that the Bible was open and a sprig of apple blossoms
lay across the pages.

It was Moses Carter's way of saying thanks.

16

Reunion

If there be a better storage place for apples than a good, dark cave, I have a hankering to know what it is. Whether the apples be bright yellow pippins, which I call God's golden pellets, big red handwarmers filled with rivers of juice, or the tough little Russets which turn from tart to sweet as they ripen, they can all be best stored in a good, dark cave.

Now that isn't to say any cave will do. Horse on a hen's egg, no! One must find such a spot and make certain it has no other creature calling it a home or storage place. A hungry brown bear can make a mighty feast of any apples you choose to put inside his shelter. And he has a right to do just that. The God of all of us provides, but we have no right to take that which is already being fairly used by another.

How many caves I've used to store apples inside I'll never know. I was glad that both the Ohio and Indiana territories always offered a good many of such containers built into the landscape. Some were small little holes, barely able to hold a good bushel of freshly picked fruit. In others, there was room for the apples from a whole orchard.

But every time I journeyed back to Ohio, I remembered little Rosey Rice. All of about twelve she was when I came upon her in one of my storage caves.

I'd been out tending the orchard nearby when I climbed the hillside leading to my favorite cave. I heard noises as I approached and I figured that some mother bear and her brood had just stopped by for an afternoon feast. Not wanting to intrude upon such a festive gathering, as sometimes bears do not appreciate guests at eating time, I was going to go about my merry way elsewhere.

But there's a speck of curiosity in me that drew me closer to the cave's entrance and I peered inside. Lo and behold, a little girl was sitting right on the floor of that cave munching one of my August delights. Farthest thing from a bear that I ever did see!

"Well, I bid you a welcome, my young miss," I offered, stepping closer with an effort not to frighten her.

The girl widened her eyes, not quite believing what she was seeing. It was not the first time my appearance gained such a surprised look. I never did see reason enough to spend a lot of time cutting my hair or trimming my beard. Some was covered up by the tin pan I wore on my head, which could easily be rinsed out and used for cooking mush. Not many folks would find a coffee sack fashionable, but with holes cut out for the head and arms, I found the garment most comfortable. Never saw much cause for wearing shoes and I was always grateful for the pantaloons some kindly farmer would trade me for appleseeds. Yes, I felt myself attired as handsome as the next man, but the look on the little girl's face did not agree with my thinking.

"No need to fear," I added, "My name is John Chapman, but some folks in these parts call me Johnny Appleseed."

The girl's face seemed to brighten a bit, as if perhaps her folks or someone had told her about me. She bit her tongue and forced herself to speak.

"My—my name is Rose," she said softly. "Roselle Rice it is really, but everyone calls me Rose."

"Ah, so we both have such names as we are, and such names as we are called. Would you like to come outside and see my trees? Are your folks hereabouts?"

"We're down by the river," she offered. "Our wagon is getting ready to cross on the next flatboat that will take us. I just decided to walk around a bit."

"Then you weren't lost?"

Rose's eyes flashed a speck of annoyance. "Hardly, Mr. Chapman—or Appleseed."

"How about Johnny?" I said. "I didn't mean any insult."

"Oh, I know, but it's just that my pa still treats me like a little girl, too, like I can never go anywhere on my own."

"Well, I'm thinking you are quite grown up. But you might not be interested in what I do in this territory. In truth, I live next door in the Indiana boundaries now, but I come back here to Ohio every year or two."

"I'd like to see your orchards, Johnny, if you don't mind showin' me. I have heard folks tell about all the trees you've planted, how it always makes settlers feel welcome to come upon some of the places you've put your seeds."

"Then come along, young lady."

The next hour passed quickly. I showed young Rose where I cleansed and sorted my appleseeds, where I started new shoots. I even helped her lift the spade and dig a hole for a planting. There was sweat on her brow, but she didn't seem to mind. A good worker she would be.

"Before you go, I'm a-gonna give you some seeds to take along with you. Now I showed you how to plant. Wherever you settle, I want you to plant those seeds. Find a place where they will get plenty of sunshine and rain. Treat them as if they were your own children. You hear me?"

"I will," Rose promised. "And thank you, Johnny."

"Don't be thanking me none, child. It's the good Lord that gives us such wondrous gifts."

Then off she ran.

Our meeting that day seldom passed my thoughts in the years that followed. Now and then I would remember little Rose whom I found in a cave, but there was much work to be done and the matter drifted away.

But six years later, on yet another trip back to Ohio from Indiana, I chanced to stop at a small handsome homestead not far from Mansfield. Behind a fine sturdy cabin were a healthy row of apple trees, standing tall and proud like angels at the entrance of heaven.

As I approached, I noticed a pretty slip of a thing churning butter on the porch. Her face seemed familiar, but I could not remember where I had seen her before.

Her memory was a mite faster than mine. "Johnny—Johnny Appleseed!" she called out, her smile covering her face.

Then I knew. It was Rose. Little Rose Rice from the cave.

"You have to stay with us tonight, Johnny Appleseed. I will make you some baked apples with

cinnamon sauce. They are apples from your very own trees. From the seeds you gave me years ago.''

And what a wonderful night it was! Rose and her parents treated me like a visiting king. I fed myself enough for a week, then opened the Bible and shared some news fresh from heaven. In the morning when I departed, Rose planted a kiss on my cheek.

''Come and visit us again,'' she said. ''You must look after your children in the back yard.''

I gazed up at the trees, swaying gently in the morning sunlight. ''I think my children are in good hands here,'' I said. ''Very good hands indeed.''

Harvest Time

A strange thing happens when a man grows older. He hits a certain point when his own meat and bones seem not to age. Each day brings the same feelings, here and there an ache or pain, but for the most part, the body stays the same. The good Lord provides a marvelous mold for a man to wear in his lifetime.

But everything else seems to get older. One notices gray hair and wrinkles among friends. The bark on young trees grows hard and gnarled. River currents wear away the shorelines. Yes, the years bring change.

Although my bare feet could still endure the rocky and hard soil, the legs to which they were attached tired more easily. The chilly breezes of winter ripped through my clothing, making me shake and shiver. And sometimes the soft whispers of the wind seem to speak my name as if a faraway voice was calling me.

But the winds carried another sound as well. The flat, even plains of Indiana were now spotted with the strong and sturdy frames of new cabins and business buildings. America was ever growing, reaching farther

and farther west. Trains rolled across the countryside. Old dusty trails carried more and more settlers. Promises of cheap land drew eager pioneers.

But for this aging pioneer, the song of westward movement was faint. My traveling days were done. The rich fertile soil of Allen County, Indiana, held me fast and firm. The days of wandering were through.

Not that the old body had completely given out. Not by a coon's nose. I could still chop kindling with men half my age, and a man need not have the spirit of a bantam hen to plant a few appleseeds.

Helping with a house raising brought back the welcome sweat of bygone days. Is there more joy than can come from using one's energies to assist another person in need? I know of none. No matter how busy the Lord was, carrying out the business of His father, He always found time to help others. If a code of living was good enough for the Lord, surely it fit the life of a humble John Chapman.

"Want to help us raise a house?" a neighbor would say. "New folks settlin' in. They'd be grateful for any spare hands."

I welcomed such invitations. True, though I knew I might not be the strongest and most able of the helpers present, none would have greater desire to assist.

Once when I was helping at such a raising and was carrying a log over a small hillside, I spotted a drift of smoke in the distance. I dropped the log, squinted out the sunlight, and centered my vision. No one knew the territory as well as I did, and I knew that was no brush fire.

"Fire!" I shouted to the others. "Fire at the Cuttler farm!"

I shot a quick look around me. A few men stood looking confused.

"I can't see nuthin," mumbled one.

"Me neither," answered another.

"Well, I can see it! Come or stay, I don't care!"

Surely the good Lord provides extra strength in times of trouble. I tore off across the field, leaving a pack of forty or so folks. Several soon took up the flight, while others stood rubbing their chins and scratching their heads.

It was the Cuttler barn that was blazing. The nearby creek was full and we put together a bucket brigade fast to pass water from the creek to the barn. There was no sign of the Cuttlers. They sometimes rode into Fort Wayne to visit relatives.

"Get that line straight!" I shouted. "Swing those buckets fast, but don't lose a drop."

We managed to save a few feed stalls in the barn,

but most of the building lay in ashes by the time the afternoon was over. Just as we were dousing the final sparks, the Cuttler family appeared in their wagon.

"How in the world—"

Ben Cuttler's voice choked a bit and I slid an arm over his shoulders to comfort him. Losing a barn was no easy matter to bear.

"Don't fret, friend," I offered. "You've got good neighbors in these parts. We'll help you build a new barn."

"You can thank Johnny Chapman here for saving your cabin and what barn is left," one of my friends said. "He saw the fire first and was the first one to get here."

"Those eyes of yours must be awful good," another neighbor said. "How old are you, Johnny?"

I straightened my frame. "Sixty-eight if you're counting years, but a lot less if you're measuring mind and spirit. Don't be pounding nails in my coffin yet, boys. I've got a bit of living to do."

My talk was sharp, but I honestly couldn't wait to get back home and soak my own feet. Scampering over fields and hauling water buckets had tired this old mule.

My travels ceased as the years slipped by. I enjoyed visiting with my friends, the Worths, on the St. Joseph River about three miles up from Fort Wayne. They always made me feel right at home, and a two-day visit easily spread into a week.

"Why, we've barely had time to visit a minute," Mrs. Worth would say when she saw me looking toward the door. "Anyway, we've got a few Johnny Appleseed tales to tell you."

Mrs. Worth knew how to hold my attention. Every time I stopped by to unwind my jaws with a little talk, she had another Johnny Appleseed tale to tell. I often wondered where such stories started.

"Some folks told us you fought a bear with your bare hands." Mrs. Worth laughed. "Right on the banks of the Maumee River."

I chuckled. "Well, if I fought a bear anywhere, I guess I would do it bare-handed!"

"Another tale came to us that you were heading west to the deserts," said William. "People say only you could grow trees in pure sand."

"I once thought I could tell a wild story," I exclaimed, "but I could never top the ones you share with me."

"But aren't any of them true?" Mrs. Worth asked.

I shook my head. "Very few, I'm afraid. Especially those that make me out to be some kind of hero. I like reading the Lord's Word and sharing it with others. I like putting seeds into the soil and watching buds turn to bushes and trees. I've been a poor man in the eyes of men, but I've felt God has showered me with many blessings in this world. I'll die happy."

"Let us not speak of death, John," Mrs. Worth suggested.

"Oh, it does not bother me," I replied. "This old body of mine is wearing down and I know it. Often I think of Ecclesiastes 12:7 where it is written: 'Then shall the dust return to the earth as it was: and the spirit shall return unto God who gave it.' Whenever the Lord is ready to call me home, I am ready to go."

"It is not for your own sake that we ask you not to speak of death," said the kind woman. "We just don't want to lose our finest boarder and favorite visitor."

Will and his wife laughed, and I joined their laughter. It was good to be with friends, people who cared and shared all with me.

The winter of 1844-45 was filled with long cold spells and heavy snows. Slowly I sensed my strength waning away. By March, I felt weak and weary. Often I thought of the days long ago—of my soldier father, of the days watching keelboats along the Connecticut, and of travels west. Now and then I dreamed the dream of my youth, of the strange woman calling to me and beckoning me to come to her. Each night, as I prayed, I ended with the same words.

"Lord, I am ready to go. Please take me with You."

Fort Wayne Sentinel—March 22, 1845

On Tuesday last, March 18, Mr. John Chapman (better known by the name of Johnny Appleseed) breathed his last breath.

John Chapman's Favorite Prayer

As John Chapman traveled westward across the heartland of America, he carried the Holy Bible with him at all times. He knew much of the Scripture by memory and shared it with thousands of pioneer families.

Of all the writings in the Holy Bible, it is said that John Chapman's favorite prayer came from Matthew 5:3-11. Many authorities claim the Beatitudes from Matthew were the final words shared by John Chapman with a family in Allen County, Indiana, shortly before he passed from this world into the next. Such an exit would be easily believable for God's faithful planter.

The Beatitudes

Blessed are the poor in spirit: for theirs is the kingdom of heaven.

Blessed are they that mourn: for they shall be comforted.

Blessed are the meek: for they shall inherit the earth.

Blessed are they which do hunger and thirst after righteousness: for they shall be filled.

Blessed are the merciful: for they shall obtain mercy.

Blessed are the pure in heart: for they shall see God.

Blessed are the peacemakers: for they shall be called the children of God.

Blessed are they which are persecuted for righteousness' sake: for theirs is the kingdom of heaven.

Blessed are ye, when men shall revile you, and persecute you, and shall say all manner of evil against you falsely, for my sake.

Did You Know . . .

- that Johnny Appleseed was the first American to be honored on the American Folklore Stamp Series issued in September, 1966?
- that the United States produces one-fourth of the world's total apple crop?
- that the cultivated apple tree is at its prime when about fifty years, and will bear fruit for over a century?
- that an apple is considered "nature's toothbrush" because its fibrous texture loosens food particles caught between the teeth?
- that apples make one of the few fruit juices whose flavor is not impaired by canning?
- that the budding and grafting of apple trees is over twenty centuries old?
- that the majority of American families buy apples at least once a week?
- that the most popular varieties of apples grown in America are Red Delicious, Golden Delicious, Rome Beauty, McIntosh, and Jonathan?
- that the Pilgrims brought appleseeds to America in 1620?
- that the minerals, nutrients, and fiber in apples help fight off illness?

Well, now you know!

Remembering
Johnny Appleseed/John Chapman

John Chapman, otherwise known as Johnny Appleseed, has been gone from the American scene for well over a century. But today there are still many tangible and intangible ways his memory lives on.

Across the heartland of the United States, memorials and monuments commemorate milestones in John Chapman's life. With silent dignity, they trace the life of God's faithful planter.

A large granite marker recognizes the site of John Chapman's birth in Leominster, Massachusetts. In nearby Springfield, an impressive monument stands in Stebbins Park.

Travelers in Ohio may follow the Johnny Appleseed Memorial Highway from Pomeroy to Toledo. Memorials have been erected in the Ohio cities of Ashland, Dexter City, and Mansfield.

Fort Wayne, Indiana, has certainly not forgotten one of its most distinguished citizens. The Johnny Appleseed Memorial Bridge spans the St. Joseph River. A granite stone marks the site of John Chapman's grave in Johnny Appleseed Memorial Park, while another granite-boulder honoring the American hero can be found in Fort Wayne's Swinney Park.

One need not travel anywhere at all to find many present reminders of John Chapman/Johnny Appleseed. Few Americans have been so often and nobly immortalized in poems, stories, plays, and songs.

Among the collection of poets who have brought Johnny Appleseed to life in words are Rosemary and Stephen Benet, Lydia Child, Allison Cooper, Frances Frost, Vachel Lindsay, Edgar Lee Masters, Carl Sandburg, and Nancy Byrd Turner.

Adult novelists who have attempted to capture the life and essence of Johnny Appleseed include Eleanor Atkinson, Louis Bromfield, Mary Catherwood, Howard Fast, Newell Hillis, and Vachel Lindsay. In the arena of children's literature, Emily Taft Douglas, Ruth Holberg, Meridel LeSeur, and Mabel Leigh Hunt have all used Johnny as the center of their accounts.

"Melody Time," a Walt Disney feature, put music to Johnny's lyrical life in 1948, and the movie still finds a receptive audience. Composers Harvey Gaul, Harvey Worthington Loomis, David Stephens, Ellie Siegmeister, and Jacque Wolfe are among those who have turned their musical talents to Johnny Appleseed.

Memorials, monuments, poems, stories, songs— all remind us of the fascinating person who was John Chapman/Johnny Appleseed. But perhaps the most impressive visual image of all are the apple blossoms and apple trees which bring beauty and richness to America. In his own lifetime, Johnny Appleseed is said to have caused fruit to be borne over a hundred thousand square miles of territory. And who will ever be able to measure the seeds of faith and hope this remarkable man sowed as he shared the Word of God with everyone he met?

Planting Apple Trees Today— Wouldn't Johnny Be Surprised?

What if Johnny Appleseed returned today? Would he feel at home in the orchards? He probably would. The apple trees are still the product of teamwork— God, nature, and man all working together.

But few of today's apple trees come from seeds like those that Johnny shared with his friends and neighbors. Trees which grow from seeds are called chance seedlings.

Apple trees are sturdy, producing a fruit that is popular all year long. Apple trees grow anywhere in the world that the proper weather is available. They thrive on sun, requiring at least a three-month period free from frost. Regular rainfall is needed, and winter temperatures must be cold enough for apple trees to shed their leaves.

Apple orchard workers spend the first months of the year pruning and trimming the trees. It is easy to spot dead and diseased branches while there are no leaves on the trees. Once the bad branches are cut off, new branches can grow. Each tree is always trimmed in a pyramid shape so that later the upper branches cannot shade the lower branches. Leaves need to share the sunlight, water, and air while they make food for the tree.

Johnny Appleseed knew it was important to watch "God's calendar" in raising apple trees. When the soil begins to dry out from winter snow, usually in April, new apple trees can be planted. These young trees have not been grown from seed. They have been grafted and budded.

Old records reveal that Johnny Appleseed did not approve of grafting and budding apple trees. But pioneer planters began the process, and today's planters continue to graft and bud.

A one-year-old apple tree is needed. For grafting, a young twig called a scion is cut from the variety of apple tree to be formed. This scion has a bud on it from which other twigs and leaves will grow. A slit is made into the tree stem and the scion is placed into it. The scion is firmly tied to the stem and a new young tree will grow from the two parts.

To bud, again a one-year-old apple tree is needed. The green bark on the stem is slit open and peeled back. A bud from the green bark of a young twig of the tree desired is slid into the open slit. The bud will grow onto the stem and a new tree will form.

Most orchard farmers plant new apple trees in the spring, but there are some who wait until autumn. Fertilizer is put into the soil to keep it rich and free from disease. As buds begin to develop into leaves, orchard farmers spray fungicides on the young trees. Fungicides help prevent such diseases as apple scab and mildew. This spraying must be done often because rain washes off the fungicide. Would Johnny Appleseed be surprised at such scientific processes? You can be sure he would!

But one time of the year in the apple orchards would not have changed since Johnny's days. In late spring the trees explode in beautiful colors. Apple blossoms of pink and white brighten the countryside. The blossoms grow in clusters of five, with the largest and first blooming blossom called the king flower. Each blossom has five petals and contains both male and female parts.

The male part of the blossom is called the stamen and there are twenty of them in the center. The stem of the stamen is called the filament. At the end of each filament is a tiny knob known as an anther.

The female part of the blossom is called the pistil. It is a thin tube protruding from the blossom's center and dividing into five smaller tubes at the top. These tubes are called style and each one has a sticky round knob at the top called a stigma. A small bulb called an ovary is located at the base of the pistil. Inside the ovary are five seed cavities known as carpels. Two tiny avules are found inside each carpel. These ovules grow into appleseeds when joined with male pollen.

How does the male pollen reach the ovules? Nature helps out here in the form of the honeybee.

The honeybee flies from blossom to blossom soaking up the sweet nectar within each flower. As the bee moves, his body picks up pollen grains from the anthers. At the next blossom, a grain may tumble off and stick to the stigma. This is called pollination. The pollen grain descends the style tube, reaches a carpel, and joins with an ovule. This process is called fertilization. When the ovules become fertilized, they grow into appleseeds. The ovary walls thicken and become the flesh of the apple. Without pollination and fertilization, tiny apples would never be born.

As soon as fertilization occurs, the petal blossoms fall. Once the blossoms are all gone, pesticides are sprayed in the orchards. These chemicals kill insects that might attack new leaves, fruit, and trees. If there are too many small apples and the branches are crowded, another chemical is sprayed to get rid of the unwanted apples. Johnny would probably shake his head in disbelief at all this spraying!

But that is the way apples are grown in orchards today. By midsummer, some varieties of apples are ripe and ready for picking. Others do not ripen until autumn.

Johnny would surely recognize the hand method of picking the apples today. Hand-picked apples are usually sold as fresh fruit. The picker wears a shoulder bag, fills it up, and then carefully empties the apples in large bins. Rough handling can cause bruises, which lessen the value and taste of the fruit.

Orchard owners who sell quantities of apples for special products like apple juice and applesauce often use big mechanical shakers. These machines knock the apples from the branches and the fruit is loaded from the ground.

Apples can be stored for a long time. Johnny kept his apples in cool caves and fruit cellars. Special refrigeration units are used today.

Yes, Johnny Appleseed would probably be very surprised at the changes in growing apple trees and harvesting apples. But one thing hasn't changed— the delicious taste of this juicy fresh fruit. Whether eaten straight from the tree, baked in a pie, sprinkled over pork chops, or diced in a salad, apples delight millions of hungry eaters.

One thing Johnny Appleseed knew—and it's still true today. God, nature, and man can truly form a wonderful team when they work together!

Johnny Appleseed's Favorite Recipes

Not all pioneers were familiar with the many nourishing uses of apples. John Chapman, affectionately called "Johnny Appleseed," always had many recipes he shared willingly. From generation to generation, these recipes have been handed down. Today's "pioneers" still enjoy these tasty treats.

Apple Butter

4 pounds apples
2 cups water
Sugar
2 teaspoons cinnamon
½ teaspoon cloves
¼ teaspoon allspice
1 tablespoon lemon juice

Wash the apples. Remove stems, cut in quarters, and cook slowly in water until apples are soft. Put fruit through a strainer. Press all the pulp through. Four pounds of apples makes 5 to 6 cups of pulp. Also add cinnamon, cloves, allspice, and lemon juice. Cook apple butter until it is thick and sheets from a spoon. Store in jars and keep refrigerated. (Back in Johnny's day, the jars were kept in the cellar or in an ice house.)

Applesauce

1 dozen apples
Water
Sugar
Lemon juice
Cinnamon

Wash, peel, core, and quarter one dozen apples, about three cups. Place in a pot and partly cover them with water. New apples need very little water, old ones need more. Stew the apples until tender, usually for an hour or more. Put them through a strainer. Season to your own taste with sugar or lemon. Sprinkle lightly with cinnamon.

Some cooks do not peel their apples. Applesauce will turn pink if the skins of red apples are stewed but strained out of the sauce. Pioneers enjoyed making applesauce both ways, but we have learned that more vitamins are retained by *not* peeling the apples.

Sweet Apple Cake

6 or more apples	1 teaspoon cinnamon
2 cups sugar	1 teaspoon vanilla
½ cup lard (or shortening)	3 cups flour
2 eggs	3 teaspoons baking powder
1¼ cups milk	½ teaspoon salt
2 tablespoons butter	1 teaspoon cream of tartar

Place a layer of apples, which have been peeled and sliced or quartered in the bottom of a greased pan. Sprinkle ½ cup of sugar and a teaspoon of cinnamon over them. Add 2 tablespoons of butter in chunks over the apples. Mix the cake batter by creaming sugar and lard, and then beating in eggs. Add milk and vanilla alternately with sifted dry ingredients. Pour over apples. Bake in a moderate oven (350 degrees) for 30 minutes or until apples and cake are done. Serve with warm milk.

Candy Apples

12 red apples
2 cups sugar

½ cup light corn syrup
¼ cup water
12 red cinnamon candies

Wash and dry apples. Put the skewer in the stem end. Mix the sugar, syrup, water, and candy in a deep saucepan. Heat until sugar is dissolved by stirring constantly. Cook until syrup becomes brittle when dropped in cold water. Remove from heat and set saucepan into boiling water to keep warm. Dip the apples into the syrup. Pull them out quickly, allowing syrup to spread evenly. Put on a rack until hard.

Pioneer Pie

Pastry for 2 crust pie
¼ to 1 cup sugar
2 tablespoons flour
½ to 1 teaspoon cinnamon
1/8 teaspoon nutmeg
¼ teaspoon salt
6 to 7 cups sliced, peeled apples (2 to 2 ½ lbs.)
2 tablespoons butter or margarine

Combine sugar, flour, cinnamon, nutmeg, and salt. Mix lightly through apples (sliced ¼ in. thick). Heap in pastry-lined 9 in. pie pan. Dot with butter. Adjust top crust and flute edges, cut vents. Bake in hot oven (425 degrees F.) 50 to 60 minutes until crust is browned.

Applehead Dolls

Many of the families John Chapman visited were poor. There were no extra pennies for "store-bought" dolls. But John knew the joy a doll could bring to girls and boys. Often he carved dollheads from apples and left them in the sun to dry. The faces became wrinkled and weathered looking. The nose, chin, and eyes could be pinched now and then to shape them.

Want to try making an applehead doll? You'll need a good healthy apple and a paring knife. (Don't forget to ask permission first!) John Chapman was handy with knives, and you must be careful, too.

Pare a firm, juicy apple as thin as possible. Remove the stem and blossom end. Carve facial features good and large. Once dried, the apple will shrink about a third. Cut eye slits about one third down from the stem end and press in a piece of peeling about the eyes to make brows. Press your thumb in to make good eye sockets. Make sure the nose sticks out as you carve. Pinch the chin and nose to form the shape you want. Don't forget to carve ears. Cut a slit for the mouth, pressing in a bit of peel if you wish. For eyes, why not press in two apple seeds?

Skewer the applehead on the end of a stick. Put it in a glass so air can circulate around and dry it out. This may take 15 to 20 days. If you want fancier bodies, use bendable wires from which you can form arms and legs.

Johnny's young friends would often simply wrap a bit of cloth around the stick and call it an applehead doll. You might like to add special effects by gluing cotton on for hair or whiskers. Appleheads are fun to paint with water colors, too.

Just remember—be careful using any knife! Johnny Appleseed always was!

BIBLIOGRAPHY

Atkinson, Eleanor. *Johnny Appleseed*. New York: Harper and Row, 1965.

Chapin, Henry. *The Adventures of Johnny Appleseed*. New York: Grosset & Dunlap, 1930.

Hunt, Mabel Leigh. *Better Known as Johnny Appleseed*. New York: J. B. Lippincott Company, 1950.

Johnson, Ann D. *The Value of Love: The Story of Johnny Appleseed*. San Diego: Oak Tree Publications, 1979.

Montgomery, Herb. *Johnny Appleseed*. Minneapolis: Winston Press, 1979.

Norman, Gertrude. *Johnny Appleseed*. New York: G. P. Putnam, 1960.

Price, Robert. *Johnny Appleseed*. Bloomington: Indiana University Press, 1954.

INDEX

SOWERS SERIES

ATHLETE
Billy Sunday, Home Run to Heaven
by Robert Allen

EXPLORERS AND PIONEERS
Christopher Columbus, Adventurer of Faith and Courage
by Bennie Rhodes
Johnny Appleseed, God's Faithful Planter, John Chapman
by David Collins

HOMEMAKERS
Abigail Adams, First Lady of Faith and Courage
by Evelyn Witter
Susanna Wesley, Mother of John and Charles
by Charles Ludwig

HUMANITARIANS
Jane Addams, Founder of Hull House
by David Collins
Florence Nightingale, God's Servant at the Battlefield
by David Collins
Teresa of Calcutta, Serving the Poorest of the Poor
by D. Jeanene Watson
Clara Barton, God's Soldier of Mercy
by David Collins

MUSICIANS AND POETS
Francis Scott Key, God's Courageous Composer
by David Collins
Samuel Francis Smith, My Country, 'Tis of Thee
by Marguerite E. Fitch